Th

The Institute of Management (IM) is at the forefront of management development and best management practice. The Institute embraces all levels of management from students to chief executives. It provides a unique portfolio of services for all managers, enabling them to develop skills and achieve management excellence.

If you would like to hear more about the benefits of membership, please write to Department P, Institute of Management, Cottingham Road, Corby NN17 1TT.

This series is commissioned by the Institute of Management Foundation.

How to Write Marketing Copy That Gets Results

. . .

JAMES ESSINGER

in the Institute
of Management
FOUNDATION
PITMAN
PUBLISHING

PITMAN PUBLISHING
128 Long Acre, London WC2E 9AN

A Division of Pearson Professional Limited

First published in Great Britain 1996

British Library Cataloguing in Publication Data
A CIP catalogue record for this book can be obtained from the British Library.

ISBN 0 273 62047 9

The author and publishers would like to thank the following for the use of copyright
material:

Hutchinson for the extracts from
The Day of the Jackal by Frederick Forsyth.

Patagonia Inc; Reed Books for the extract from
Writing a Novel by John Braine.

10 9 8 7 6 5 4 3 2 1

Typeset by Northern Phototypesetting Co Ltd, Bolton
Printed and bound in Great Britain by Bell and Bain Ltd, Glasgow

The Publishers' policy is to use paper manufactured from sustainable forests.

For Sandy

'O brave new world,
That has such people in 't!'

Contents

■ ■ ■

v

Preface

■ ■ ■

This is a practical book offering practical guidance on writing marketing copy that gets results: that is, awakens and sustains the reader's interest and makes him or her willing to absorb whatever sales or corporate message you wish to communicate.

My overall aim is principally a commercial one. However, a lesson in writing good marketing copy must inevitably also be a lesson in writing well generally. In many respects, then, this book constitutes a general guide to good writing.

To what extent can the skill of writing well be taught? We are apt to view it with reverence, as if it were something one is either born with or not. My view is that more of this skill can be taught than is usually realised. It is even possible to learn how to write with flair, and I try to suggest how to do this where appropriate. Overall, my advice constitutes a mixture of general guidance and specific blueprints and frameworks.

I make no apologies for quoting almost as many examples from the world of literature as from the world of marketing: the works of the masters have a great deal to teach us. Examples are used throughout the text: they are numbered and listed at the back of the book.

The possession of first-rate writing skills is already an important part of the matrix of management expertise, and can only become more important in the future. It has never been sensible for a manager automatically to offload the job of writing marketing copy to a member of his organisation's staff, or to an external writer or agency. In today's business climate the case for managers to do the job themselves – or at the very least understand enough to be able to revise other people's drafts effectively – has never been stronger.

I describe something of my own experience as a writer in the Introduction; for the moment it is enough to mention that I have been a practising public relations consultant and business writer since 1984. During this time I have published numerous business books and full-length consultancy reports, as well as writing a wide range of marketing copy for organisations in the United Kingdom, United States and in Western and Central Europe – including many of the top 100 corporations in these geographical regions.

Starting a High-income Consultancy, the other book I have published in this Pitman/Institute of Management series, was fun to write and appears to have been well received. Publishing it placed me in the unfamiliar position of receiving appreciative letters and phone calls from readers. The remit of *Writing Marketing Copy That Gets Results* is much wider than that of *Starting a High-income Consultancy*, but I hope that in addition to having this more general appeal, it will also be helpful to those who found *Starting a High-Income Consultancy* a useful introduction to consultancy life.

I am grateful to Tom Rayfield, a director of the leading international advertising agency J. Walter Thompson, who was most generous with advice and guidance for the chapters on writing sales letters and advertising copy: the only two areas of marketing writing in which I do not have extensive personal experience.

I would also like to extend my thanks to Richard Stagg, my publisher at Pitman Professional, for his initiation of this project and his intelligent enthusiasm for it; to Amelia Lakin, also of Pitman Professional, for her friendly assistance and suggestions; to Julian Goldsmith, managing director of Sector Public Relations, London, who supplied a most useful exhibit and who has always been a good friend and fellow writer of marketing copy; to Frankie Thornhill (who became Frankie Cooper while this book was in preparation) for information about Chinese; to Tara Connolly of the library of Lincoln College, Oxford, for hunting down the Edward Gibbon quotation; to Andy Bainbridge of Barclays Global Securities Services for permission to reproduce an issue of *The Custodian*; and to John Dembitz for allowing me to use the corporate brochure of IDOM Consultants.

I would also like to thank my clients, who have allowed me to enjoy the privilege of earning my living as a professional writer.

James Essinger
Canterbury

Introduction:
What you can expect
from this book

■ ■ ■

How to Write Marketing Copy That Gets Results is a bold and ambitious title for a bold and ambitious book.

My aim is that by the time you reach the end of it, you will have been exposed to a wide range of general and specific guidance on how to write marketing copy which is a complete knock-out.

Along the way I will set myself the task of entertaining you, challenging you when I think you might enjoy a challenge, forcing you to stretch yourself mentally when the problem in question demands it, and above all keeping you reading.

Above all keeping you reading. Exactly. In essence, the challenge facing me in this book is the same challenge which faces you in writing marketing copy: **to keep your readers interested and to keep them reading**.

What is marketing copy?
■ ■ ■

What exactly do I mean by 'marketing copy'? I include the following types of writing within this umbrella term:

- Press releases and other types of material directed at obtaining press coverage, including full-length articles.
- Business literature, including sales literature.
- Sales letters.

- Speeches and presentations.
- Advertising copy.

The challenge to be interesting
■ ■ ■

It is a sweeping statement that the primary and most important objective of writing marketing copy is to keep the reader reading, but it is also profoundly true and absolutely fundamental to all that follows. **As a writer of marketing copy, your main challenge is to be as interesting as you possibly can**. Of course you have commercial objectives, too, but none of these has a chance of being fulfilled if your work isn't interesting enough for the reader to read on.

Your job is to be interesting, so you must avoid falling into the following traps.

One of the most common mistakes is to imagine you have **a captive readership whom you can bombard with pompous statements about how good your organisation/firm/product is**. Promoting your organisation/firm/product is a fine and laudable aim, but the sooner you discard any idea that your readership is in any way captive, the better. There's no such thing as a captive readership for marketing copy, unless perhaps we're talking about new recruits who are desperate to make an impression, or interviewees who read your corporate brochure in the lobby. Almost anybody else – pretty well *everybody else*, in fact – will need a reason for reading on, and the only reason for reading on is that the reader finds the writing interesting.

Another mistake is simply to **provide a mass of raw information, which readers are free to deal with as they like**: if you want to be a top-class writer of marketing copy you must accept right away that your job is to impose order on chaos; not create more chaos by setting down raw, unanalysed, unpresented, unfocused, unguided information. Even a telephone directory imposes some measure of order on chaos by conveniently putting the listings into alphabetical sequence.

As a writer you are a lone individual standing on the shore of a vast ocean of words; your job is to select the ones you want, impose a pleasing and interesting order on them, and not, for one moment, be even slightly intimidated by the existence of that great ocean. If you seek a potent image for the job of the writer, think of yourself as a verbal Neptune: the God of the sea of words, with your pen, typewriter or word processor the trident with which you tame the roaring swell of chaotic verbiage, and conquer the giant octopus of cliché, the sharks of the common-place and the barracuda of repetition.

As a writer you have to be responsible for organising your words and your material, and if you think that's a trivial responsibility, it isn't. The great writer Ernest Hemingway (who, apart from being a first-class novelist, was also a fine journalist) often used to speak of the responsibility that goes with writing, and he was right. Finally, **don't imagine that good marketing copy is a trivial part of your organisation's bid for success.** If you don't believe the quality of the marketing copy your organisa-tion publishes and projects to its existing, potential and possible customers is a major element of its activities and a crucial part of your attempt to win competitive advantage, for goodness' sake pass the writing task to someone who does.

On the other hand, if you *are* worried at the notion that your marketing copy must, first and foremost, be interesting, that's good, because you'll be receptive to my next premise, which is that while it isn't easy to write amazing, absorbing, top-quality marketing copy, you *can* learn to write that kind of copy. But you must be prepared to work at it.

Why write marketing copy yourself?

■　■　■

At this point you might ask: yes, but why should I go to all that trouble? Why shouldn't I simply delegate the task of writing marketing copy to someone else?

On the face of it, there's no reason why you shouldn't. But con-sider the following points:

- **Anybody wanting to excel in business should be able to excel at writing marketing copy**: as business guru Charles Handy has pointed out, we live in a business climate where life-long careers are largely a thing of the past. Handy argues that people who want to get ahead now need a portfolio of special skills rather than traditional career qualifications. Common sense suggests that a business skill as important as the ability to write good marketing copy ought to be part of that portfolio.

In any case, how effective can anybody possibly be in an organisation if they can't express in writing what makes their organisation special?

My own experience in business has convinced me that the ability to write good marketing copy is an essential part of the skills matrix of any ambitious executive, and will often prove a major factor not only in career advancement within a particular corporation, but also in getting the right job within that corporation in the first place.

- **The nature of the business world today makes correct presentation ever more crucial to success**: in an increasingly competitive, international and fast-moving business environment, success is (sadly, perhaps) often as much about correct presentation as it is about successful delivery. First-class marketing copy is an essential part of correct presentation.

- **The importance of marketing copy as a tool to promote your company makes it imperative that senior management should keep a firm control over it**: the role of marketing copy as a competitive weapon has never been more important. It is essential senior management realise and understand the need to give it top priority, which in practice means exercising firm control over it.

Note that this applies whether you are running a one-person business, a medium-sized business or a multinational.

- **Many senior managers will want to write marketing copy themselves**: increasingly, senior management, aware that someone remote from the management process may not know enough of the organisation's approach and strategy, prefer to have this ultimate level of control. And even where they do not write the copy themselves they will always – or should always – want to have full control over the revision process.

By the term 'senior management' here I mean the highest echelons of management of *any* organisation.

■ **Using an external writer often has serious drawbacks:** as someone who makes part of his income from writing marketing copy for a wide range of commercial organisations, I ought to be more in favour of using an external writer than I am. However, whereas – for reasons I explain later in this book – I think it makes a great deal of sense to use an external writer for producing advertising copywriting, I tend to believe that organisations should avoid contracting out their marketing copy unless absolutely unavoidable: that is, if nobody at the organisation has any idea how to write the marketing copy, or if the job is a specialised one – such as the production of a technical promotional article – which nobody in-house is able to write in a reasonable time-frame.

xv

If neither of these applies, you are in most cases better off doing the job yourself, for the following reasons:

■ **Using an external writer is expensive.** Most freelance writers will charge about £300 per day, and editorial agencies or public relations consultancies (many of which simply farm their work out to freelancers and rake off the profit) will charge up to about £600 a day, or even more.

■ **The external writer may not produce good work.** The production of good marketing copy is so important for an organisation that within reason the cost of producing it is likely to be justified *if the work which the external writer produces is first-rate*. The trouble is that often this is not the case. This is not necessarily the writer's fault. While there are some freelance writers who are less good at what they do than they ought to be, a more usual cause of poor quality work is that the writer has been inadequately briefed.

Inadequate briefs given to external writers generally stem from two causes:

a) The client could not be bothered to brief the writer properly.

b) The client is unsure what the precise nature of the brief should be. My own experience has convinced me this problem is the more common of the two. All too often, clients do not know what kind of marketing copy they want; and even when they do know, have little idea of the style or tone they require. Unfortunately, while external writers will (or should be) competent verbal technicians, they won't be mind-readers. Unless the client is able to communicate in broad terms what the principal contents and approach should be, it's difficult to see how the resulting copy can be satisfactory.

Of course, this problem of the inadequate brief also occurs *within* an organisation, when a senior manager fails to communicate to a writer within an in-house public relations or marketing department what is required. However, this problem will usually be easier to solve, because the public relations or marketing department will most likely have a hand in compiling the brief in the first place, and it is easier to rectify an internal communications problem than one involving an outsider.

- **For reasons of confidentiality, the organisation may not want to reveal anything about its forthcoming marketing copy to any external party.** Typical reasons for this include the desire to retain a hard-won competitive edge, and those occasions where the organisation is bound by statute or regulation to maintain confidentiality – such as where it is a public company and the marketing copy will reveal price-sensitive information.

An organisation can get around this by using an external writer or agency with experience in working on a strictly confidential basis, but many organisations will nonetheless prefer to keep the information securely in-house.

For these reasons, I believe it is important to understand how to write effective marketing copy.

And, when you have mastered writing marketing copy, you will find the copy you write gets results by achieving most, or all, of the following objectives:

- Keeping your readers interested from start to finish.
- Convincing your readers of your point of view.
- Making your readers want to buy whatever it is you have to sell.

- Exciting your readers and making them remember your organisation or your products and services long after they have forgotten your rival's organisation and *its* products and services.

Are good writers born or made?
■ ■ ■

By now you might be thinking: *all right, so I know what you're aiming to do for me in this book and I can see that mastering the writing of marketing copy will be a real boost to my business career, but I'm still not convinced the ability to write well can be taught.*

Yes, some people may at a very basic level have more inherent writing ability than others, but we're not talking here about writing brilliant poetry, or novels, or other types of creative work, we're talking about writing marketing copy: a serious challenge, certainly, but not an impossibly difficult one.

I suggest that, instead of wondering whether or not you have any talent for writing marketing copy, you reflect that all those who excel at it have had to learn through sheer hard work and constant practice. This applies even to those who have started with some kind of innate ability; indeed, it probably applies *even more* to them, because their sense of having some inherent flair may have lulled them into the false belief that they can write easily, and that what they write with such facility will be splendid. In fact, the chances are it won't be.

I speak from personal experience. Without wishing to appear arrogant, I knew from early on in my childhood that I'd been born with at least some ability to write. I was almost always top of the class in 'English' (which was principally composition) at school. I wrote for the school magazine and wrote a play at the age of 14 which was performed in front of several hundred pupils. At the age of 19 I wrote an essay for a leading bank's essay competition and won £50: a sum that seemed enormous in 1976. I studied English at Oxford University and never had any real doubt that after leaving university I would be a 'writer'.

When I did leave university I wasn't sure how to make a living from writing, so I spent three years teaching English in Finland, instead. While there, I wrote two novels and a book of short stories. I posted these with a sort of naïve optimism to publishers in England, and a month or so later the publishers posted them back. After returning to England in 1984 I managed to find a job at a small public relations consultancy, where I had my first taste of business writing. I was still writing novels, too. The typical start of a promising career? Not exactly, no. There's only one word for the quality of the work I was producing at work and in my spare time: abysmal. Here was I, supposedly a typical 'talented' writer, and I didn't know how to write. In theory I should have done, but I didn't.

It was only two years later, after working at business writing for an average of about six hours a day most weekdays, that I started to produce work which clients were prepared to use without significant revision.

In 1987, I wrote a long report on cash machines. This became my first full-length publication. A year later, on the way to work, I had an idea for another, more ambitious, business report. I stopped at the next public phone box, telephoned the publisher who had brought out the cash machine report and told him I wanted to write a report about the role computers had played in the 1987 global stock market crash. I said if I was going to do it I would need to give up my job and devote myself to the project full-time. He agreed to give me an advance which, while far from being a king's ransom, would allow me to live for about six months without starving. I thanked him, put the phone down, went to the office where I worked and handed in my notice.

I wrote the report, it did reasonably well, and since then I have worked as a self-employed writer and journalist. I've published twenty-two full-length business-related publications. These range from expensive management reports costing £350 per copy to mass market books like this one, costing a great deal less. At the moment (August 1995), as well as writing this book, I'm also writing a thriller about virtual reality, a popular (well, I hope it will be, anyway) book about the future of computers, and am working on various writing projects for clients who include a New York investment bank, a UK clearing bank, a financial information vendor and a computer software house. On the face of it I've gone some modest way to fulfilling the 'promise' I showed when younger.

But what I've been conscious of in the years since I began working as a full-time freelance writer is the daily grind of the business of writing; of trying to find the right words; of thinking of ideas and approaches and then ditching most of them because they don't have the required effect; of revising my work and often choosing different words to express what I thought I'd already expressed well enough, but on second reading discovered I hadn't.

The point is, I had to teach myself to write. And, yes, it *is* something you can learn. More than that: it *has* to be something you can learn, because it's such a complex skill there's absolutely no way you can be born with it.

True: there is an element of art, of flair, in all good writing which can't readily be taught. But – and it's a big but – writing is a science, too, and there is far more about writing which *can* be taught than most people believe. There are rules, procedures and guidelines about using words and grammar, which certainly can be learnt, and which you really do need to know if you are to write effective marketing copy. You'll still need flair, but if you learn the nuts and bolts of writing, it's a fair chance that will come of its own accord.

Ken Follett, one of the most successful novelists in the world – and, incidentally, an excellent writer of the marketing copy, press releases, biographical details and dust-jacket blurbs his publishers use to sell his books around the globe – is famous within the writing fraternity for the application he brings to his task. He revises his books with infinite care until he gets the words right; he invites comments on his work from a wide range of family members and friends before he even thinks of showing it to his agent; he starts work early in the morning and never touches anything to do with the business side of writing until four in the afternoon. And if you imagine that careful reworking and revision of a book will produce flat, uninspired material, read his superb thriller *Eye of the Needle* and change your mind.

Ah, but he's a novelist, you say, *and I'm just trying to write marketing copy*. Yes, but as a writer of marketing copy you have something in common with Mr Follett and with every novelist who ever lived: like them, as I have already pointed out, your overriding duty is to be interesting.

So that is the main challenge which faces you. Now let's look at how you can meet it, as well as meet the other challenges involved in writing first-rate marketing copy.

1
■ ■ ■

You, the writer

The importance of professionalism
Difficulties of writing for strangers
The written language: how does it work?
Fundamental rules of writing
Writing tools: advantages and disadvantages

Commitment and professionalism

■ ■ ■

To be a good writer you have to take your writing seriously. This doesn't mean you necessarily need to be a full-time writer who focuses on writing to the exclusion of any other activity – in fact, this book is as much for people who specialise in some other area as for those who want to write marketing copy full-time – but it does mean that while you are writing, you commit yourself to carrying out your writing with the utmost professionalism.

That point is obvious enough, but it needs making, all the same. The problem is that writing is something which anybody who is literate can, by definition, do. We live in an age where most people in developed countries *are* literate, and since most of us write something or other every day, even if it's only a shopping list or a memo, it's too easy to assume that any kind of more disciplined, formal writing, is just an extension of what we do every day.

In fact, it isn't. When you write marketing copy you are writing for strangers. This is a far cry from writing for yourself (such as a shopping list or an entry in a diary) or for people who know you.

The special demands of writing for strangers

■ ■ ■

Writing for strangers is the most difficult kind of writing, because strangers are, by definition, people who:

- Probably don't care about you personally in the least.
- Don't necessarily care about your organisation and its products or services.
- May not be particularly willing to read your marketing copy in the first place, and won't read on at all unless they find it rivetting.
- Are constantly being bombarded with other written visual/aural material which demands their attention.
- Are probably busy.
- Are easily bored.

2

In other words, writing for strangers is tough. It's difficult even if you *do* adopt a professional and committed attitude; if you *don't*, it's likely to be impossible. And make no mistake, it's a profession where you never stop learning, although you may well be able to produce readable and effective material relatively soon after you start the learning process.

Oh, yes, a year or so (or even a few months) after producing that material you'll look back on it and wonder how you could have written so badly, but that's a positive sign, because it means you're getting better.

All good writers have two fundamental points in common: they're rarely entirely satisfied with their work even when they're writing it, and when they look back on it some time later they're even less satisfied. But this is different from never releasing their writing for public consumption. Good writers know that ultimately all writing is a compromise – the compromise of execution against intention. They know they will always in some sense fail when they write, but they are brave enough to be judged by the strength of their failures, and professional enough to know that a writer who doesn't at some point release work for public consumption isn't a writer at all.

3

So, yes, you certainly ought to be awed by the prospect of writing for indifferent and easily bored strangers, but you also ought to be courageous enough to realise that when you've done your best – and I *mean* your best, not some half-baked drivel you tossed off in twenty minutes before that lunch meeting – you shouldn't be afraid of showing it to the wider world.

In this chapter I suggest certain general precepts to follow in order to get yourself into what might be termed the 'write frame' of mind: the mindset where you *are* likely to do your very best writing. In subsequent chapters I look at structure and style, and at the challenges posed by writing specific types of marketing copy.

Let's start in the most logical way: by focusing on what exactly writing is in the first place.

The written language
■ ■ ■

A formal definition of writing would be to call it **a form of human communication which uses a set of visible marks that are related, by accepted convention, to a spoken language**. This definition is a useful one; it teases out four major points about writing that need to be identified right away.

Writing is a form of communication

Writing to 'express yourself' or to come to terms with some personal problem or difficulty is all very well, but the real point of writing is to communicate something to one's fellow human beings.

Writing uses a set of visible marks

We are so familiar with the written form of language we rarely reflect that writing is nothing more or less than marks on some kind of medium which will accommodate the mark with (probably) a degree of permanence.

Writing is an accepted convention

This point follows logically from the principle that writing is a form of communication. Obviously, where you want to communicate something to another person in a more subtle way than simply chucking a clod of earth at them, you and the recipient of your message must have the same terms of reference. If you don't, the message won't be understood by the recipient.

In fact, the kind of accepted convention that writing involves is a doubly complex one, because writing is a conventional depiction of a spoken language, and a spoken language is itself an accepted convention. In order to use writing as a form of communication, you and your reader must share the same spoken language *and* the marks you make must conform to the convention your reader understands.

It is important to bear in mind that both these conventions are purely arbitrary: that is, they only work because there is agreement among the speakers of a particular language about which sounds have which meaning, and among writers and readers of that spoken language about which marks relate to which sounds or elements of meaning in the spoken language.

The qualification 'or elements of meaning' is necessary here because, while in English and in all alphabetical languages, writing mainly refers to the sounds of the spoken language, this isn't invariably the case.

For example, the symbolic forms of the cardinal numbers 1, 2, 3, 4 and so on are conventional depictions of the *meaning* these numbers have: you can of course also write them as 'one', 'two', 'three', 'four' and so on, but there you *would* be representing the sounds rather than the meaning.

The English symbol known as the ampersand (&) is another example of a written symbol which refers to the *meaning* of the concept 'and' rather than how the word 'and' is pronounced.

However, symbols which relate to meaning are extremely rare in English, as in all alphabetical languages. The whole idea of an alphabet is that it provides a way of representing all the sounds of a language with a relatively small number of conventional symbols (i.e. letters).

5

Readers are so familiar with letters that they prefer to see them whenever they can. This is why writing, for example, 'selling & marketing' is usually regarded as less acceptable than 'selling and marketing': the sound-reference symbols are seen as better usage than the meaning-reference symbols.

With other languages it is a different story. In Chinese, for example, the characters have the same function as the symbols '&' or '£': that is, they refer to meanings rather than sounds. Originally Chinese characters were pictograms: diagrammatic pictures visually representing the thing or idea to which they refer, but the vast majority of Chinese characters are nowadays purely stylised conventions and give no obvious visual clues to what they mean. If you can't read Chinese, you can't understand them. There are a few exceptions: for example the character which means 'person', has the forked appearance of a human being, and the one which means 'tree', looks something like one. However, Chinese characters are, in the main, an arbitrary system of signs: their meaning depends on a convention and cannot be ascertained merely from looking at them.

Incidentally, English is a remarkably inefficient alphabetical language. It's difficult to know how to pronounce an English word unless you've learnt how to pronounce it: you can't easily guess. It's just as difficult to know how to spell an English word unless you've learnt the spelling: improvisation rarely works.

Learning to spell English is a nightmare. Words such as 'knight', 'night', 'plough', 'cough', 'island', 'guess', 'rhythm', 'photograph' and thousands of others are not at all spelt as you would expect. Why is this? There are three main reasons.

- English sounds are not inherently well suited to the Latin alphabet (witness the crude way the letters 'th' represent the sound at the start of the words 'these' and 'thin').

- English spelling became fixed several hundred years ago; the pronounciation of English has changed (for example, Geoffrey Chaucer pronounced 'night' as 'nicht', as the Germans still do).

- The thousands of words English has borrowed from other languages have generally, for reasons of clarity of meaning, retained their original spelling while their pronunciation has changed.

Still, for all its eccentricities, English is sufficiently phonetic for the alphabet to offer readers the huge advantage of having to learn to recognise only twenty-six letters. And fortunately, while there are many words we will never learnt to spell except by hard work, there are many words where the spelling rules are relatively simple.

But the price we pay for using an alphabet is that there can be no possible way of guessing the meaning of a word from its appearance on the page: the system is purely arbitrary. Spoken language is to a large degree arbitrary, too; we can't generally guess what a word means from the sound of it.

Some years ago, when the Rolls-Royce company was looking for a new name for its cars, it hit on the idea of 'Silver Mist'. How could a word as pleasant to the ear as 'mist' – which might be said to have a frailty and fragility in its sound evocative of gentle morning mist rising off a field of Scottish heather on a summer dawn – be anything but beautiful? Plans for the new name were well advanced when a horrified distributor in Germany – a major market for Rolls-Royce – pointed out that, in German, 'Mist' means 'excrement'.

Writing relates to a spoken language

There are many languages without written forms, but no languages without spoken forms.

In order that the largest number of speakers can understand the written form of a language, writing has to adopt standardised spellings of words which may be pronounced in a quite different way by different speakers. A London aristocrat and a Glaswegian dock-worker will say, 'I'm having a bath and then I'll watch the football on television, Jimmy', in very different ways, but they can both read the words on the page.

Quite apart from regional variations, many families, social groups, or communities with a shared interest have words which are peculiar to themselves and/or have a special meaning peculiar to themselves. These words are readily understood by the family, social group or community and must be seen as part of the English they speak. Often these words have neither standardised spellings nor familiar meanings. One of the most popular books published in Britain during the early 1990s was the diary of the former cabinet minister Alan Clark. Beautifully written, the diary contained numerous Clark family words which had to be defined in footnotes in order to be comprehensible.

We often forget how many regional variations remain even in modern English. I come originally from the Midlands, where common dialect words were 'mardy', meaning 'sulky', and 'narked' meaning 'annoyed, cross'. When I moved south I stopped using these words because nobody understood them.

My spellings for 'mardy' and 'narked' are all examples of non-standard English spellings for which there is no accepted convention. Conversely, standardised spellings cover a wide range of different pronounciations of the same word. These standardised spellings are a force in reducing dialect variation, but written language remains a compromise for the recording of spoken language. And, once the compromise has been painstakingly learnt by the language speaker (that is, once the speaker has learnt how to spell) the speaker, quite understandably, does not

7

want to have to re-learn the job, which is why – even though the way in which a language is pronounced will change over time due to mistakes by speakers and the desire to say words as quickly as possible – the written form of a language is highly conservative.

Rules of writing

■ ■ ■

These elements, which define what writing is, lead directly to four fundamental rules that should govern your writing. These are as follows:

1. The primary aim of writing is to communicate something to your reader

What precisely you will be communicating depends on what you are writing. In the case of marketing copy, you may want to communicate any or all of the following messages:

- The overall excellence of your organisation.
- The great attention your organisation pays to meeting customer needs.
- The excellence of the products and/or services your organisation supplies.
- Your organisation's position as a leading player, or *the* leading player, in its industry.
- The high levels of professionalism of your colleagues.
- Your organisation's dynamic future plans.
- The continuing development of the products and/or services your organisation supplies.

I examine the general principles of *how* you communicate these messages later in this chapter. For the moment, the point to remember is that **a message is indistinguishable from the medium in which the message is sent**.

Think of your writing as if it were an arrow, and this point will be clear. The purpose of firing an arrow at some person or an animal is to inflict physical damage on them or it: in effect the 'message' conveyed by an arrow is dislike, anger, hatred, hunger (you might be hunting for food), excitement (you might be hunting for fun) or fear. But the 'message' will only be an effective one if the arrow is correctly shaped, correctly flighted (i.e. the feathers at its end are regularly configured and will give a true flight) and if its point is sharp. If any of these technical requirements is lacking, the arrow will not strike its target, or will not be effective when it does.

Note that the message which the arrow is conveying is in no way distinct from its technical aspects. If the arrow fails to hit the target, or strikes the target ineffectively, your dislike/anger/ hatred/hunger/excitement/fear **will not be conveyed by the physical impact of the arrow**. Of course, if your target is a person who saw you firing the arrow at them, that person would certainly be able to draw some conclusion about how you felt about them, but this doesn't affect the point I'm making, which is that – as the American social theorist Marshall McLuhan has said – **the medium is the message**.

The writing which aims to communicate the message you are seeking to convey is *not* something additional to the message or something that conceals the message, it *is* the message. If your writing is forceful, dramatic and sharp, your message will be forceful, dramatic and sharp. Conversely, if your writing is weak, uninteresting and flat, your message will be weak, uninteresting and flat.

9

Here are two examples to demonstrate this point.

✍ EXAMPLE 1

The slogan *Players Please* was one of the most popular and successful slogans in marketing history. It is such a sharp, pert, clever slogan that – quite apart from anything else – it has overcome my reluctance to quote a slogan which was used to market cigarettes.

The slogan gains its force from its succinctness and its ambiguity: *Players Please* is not only a concise way of saying *Players' cigarettes provide pleasure* but is also a statement of what a Players' customer would say to his tobacconist. The slogan would not be as effective today as it was in the past, because the use of the word 'please' as a verb, while still readily understood, is no longer common.

Consider if, instead of being 'Players Please' the slogan had been *Players Please People, And 'Players Please' Is What The Shrewd Customer Says When Visiting His (Or Her) Tobacconist.*

Can there be any doubt that the longer slogan has none of the punch and impact of the original, and that therefore its message is far less strong, even if it says the same thing?

✍ EXAMPLE 2

My other example is from literature. The following sentence is a clumsy paraphrase of one of the most famous first lines of a Shakespearian sonnet. Be Shakespeare for a moment, and try to work out what the Bard actually wrote. The paraphrase is:

> *Would it be in my interest to effect a comparison between you and any unspecified twenty-four hour period that occurs at or around the summer solstice?*

10

Twenty-six tedious words; before reading on see whether you can do better.

In fact, Shakespeare did it in eight words which nobody is likely easily to forget. What he wrote was:

> *Shall I compare thee to a summer's day?*

Is there any doubt Shakespeare's version carries the sentiment with infinitely more energy and vigour than my (admittedly absurd) longer version?

It follows that the better your writing, the more effective your message will be. There are no exceptions to this fundamental principle.

You can't turn bad writing into good writing by piling on the words, or by using italics, or by getting your design department to excel themselves creatively. You can't create good writing by any other means than by writing well.

2. Your finished writing must be free from errors

The sheer technical quality of your writing is one thing, and this whole book is about how to maximise it, but you must also bear in mind that writing has a physical existence as marks on paper or on some other medium. An important part of your profession-alism as a writer is to ensure that the technical presentation of those marks is of the highest standard. And while, ultimately, the quality of all writing will be a matter of opinion, the quality of the marks on the paper can be assessed perfectly objectively.

As a writer, therefore, it is your job to ensure all of the following:

■ **That your writing contains no spelling mistakes:** there really is no excuse for these whatsoever. Dictionaries are freely to hand, and many word processors contain built-in spellcheck programs. Yes, I know that *paralell* lines still meet at infinity and that you can have a good night's rest in *accomodation* (just for the record, the correct spellings are *parallel* and *accommoda-tion*) but if you can't be bothered to spell your work properly, your readers are entitled to ask why they should bother to read it, let alone be swayed by what you have to say.

■ **That your writing contains no errors in punctuation:** there's no excuse for these, either, even though I admit that punctuating English is more difficult than most people believe. There are many important rules about punctuation, but there are also many grey areas, where the use of punctuation is an art rather than a science.

In the next chapter I look in detail at spelling and punctuation.

■ **That your writing contains no 'typos':** the typo, or typo-graphical error, is a particular problem in today's business writing environment, where it is common for writing to be pre-pared on a personal computer and printed by a desk-top pub-lishing system. It is all too easy for an error to persist throughout every stage of the writing and revising process and to appear in the final, published text.

Obviously, the farther the typo persists along the road to publi-cation, the more serious a threat it is to the quality of the work. It is particularly important that typos are removed from proofs (i.e. a final draft of the writing that has been prepared by the typesetter or publisher for last-minute checking). I tend to the belief that the earlier in the process the typo is removed, the better, which is a genteel way of saying that any writer who pro-duces work which contains typos is at best unprofessional, and at worst an idiot. The only sensible approach to adopt towards typos is to get rid of them as soon as you can, and certainly by the time you are onto the second draft.

(Of course, I realise only too well that you will now no doubt jump for joy if you find a typo in this book).

There are three major kinds of typos, namely:

■ **The unintentional spelling mistake:** this occurs when the writer knows how to spell a word but accidentally presses the wrong key and misspells it. For obvious reasons, the incorrect letter or letters that feature in the word are usually located on the keyboard close to the letters that should appear.

We all have our own favourite spelling typos. One of mine is *comnputer* for 'computer'. Also, I often manage to write *ythe* for 'the', as well as *koind* for 'kind'.

Fortunately this ko – sorry, kind of typo usually looks so outrageous that it is easy to spot.

■ **The wrong word being accidentally used:** this occurs when the writer's concentration has momentarily slipped, or when he is thinking about something (or someone) else. It is surprising how often words creep into writing which don't belong there at all.

Usually these typos are easy to spot, as they are so preposterous. The problem arises when they are not so preposterous, which is all too often the case when the word is relatively short and inconspicuous. The words 'of' and 'or' are a particular problem here, as are 'is' and 'if'. These words are frequently interchanged with one another, with the incorrect word being surprisingly difficult to spot.

■ **Residual typos resulting from text being revised on a word processor's screen:** a common kind of typo occurs when written work has been revised on a word processor's screen (whether or not after scrutiny in hard copy form) and text has been cut or added with insufficient attention to the appearance of the new version.

Residual typos are usually found at the beginning or end of sentences, when the sentence has been revised in the middle but not checked to make sure that it starts and ends accurately. Of the two positions, residual typos tend to predominate at the *end* of sentences, with the typo often consisting of excess punctuation.

Fortunately, all typos are easy to avoid, given that you take the trouble to get rid of them. If you are using a typewriter, the only way to avoid them is to take care as you go and correct your work as you proceed. On the other hand, if you are using a word processor, typos can be avoided by the relatively straightforward expedient of printing out your work and *then* reading it through carefully for typos. *Printing your work out before checking for typos is always much more effective than checking for typos on the screen.* I don't know why this should be the case, but it is.

Even so, there is a danger some typos will remain in your work after your intent scrutiny. This is because your brain will already have 'marked' some typos as correct, when they are not. Be aware that – as I have already mentioned – this is particularly likely with short words that are wrong but not misspelt. It is for this reason that when checking over a proof you should always get someone else to check it with you, and ideally get them to read out what they read. Reading out aloud is an infallible way to spot a typo that has been missed so far.

3. Your writing must follow the principal rules of writing

As writing is a convention, you must follow the rules of the convention if you are to be understood. This does not mean you cannot break some of them in order to achieve a particular effect, but before you can break the rules you must know them.

4. Your writing must come across as the spoken language, written down

Generally, the only good writing is writing that reads like the spoken language sounds. In other words, your writing must have the same conciseness, fluency and energy as the most expressive spoken language.

When we speak we usually find it fairly easy to be concise, fluent and energetic because we have something we need to communicate with a certain amount of urgency. When we write, unless we are desperate to communicate something urgently (such as the message 'I love you', written on a slip of paper), we rarely have such an immediate and urgent need to communicate.

13

The result is that our writing easily becomes flabby and long-winded. We use formal words instead of short, punchy words; we use long, winding sentences; we use more words than we need to; we put all sorts of unhelpful dependent clauses and qualifications into our writing.

I don't know why so many people – including highly intelligent businesspeople who are direct, even aggressive, in their everyday business lives – have so many problems understanding that good writing must read like written spoken language, not like some laborious, formal, stylised 'writing'. The words should jump off the page into the reader's face: good writing really should be that alive.

It's especially puzzling why so many otherwise intelligent people write so laboriously and formally, because the secret of making your writing read like spoken language is really very simple. As there is (probably) no inherent urgency in the message you are communicating through your writing, you must 'build in' an urgency, which means that at all times when you are writing, **you must think of yourself as communicating what you want to say urgently, simply and economically**.

We've now examined in some detail what writing is and what general rules your writing should follow. Let's now start focusing on the writing process in greater detail, and start talking about specifics rather than generalities. Since we are now moving onto the day-to-day job of writing, it clearly makes sense to start with the tools you use to do your writing.

14

Writing Tools
■ ■ ■

There are three main types of writing tool. I list these in the chronological order of their invention.

1. Pen and ink

This is not of course the oldest type of writing tool, but I don't see much to be gained by discussing the stylus or the etching tool that was used to write cuneiform, so pen and ink will do as a starting-point.

Pen and ink have the great advantages of being easy to use anywhere, easily preserved unless you lose the paper, and – as long as you write legibly – easy to read.

I rather tend to the view that in our high-tech world, where many of us (or probably most of us) do much or all of our business writing with high-tech tools, it's too easy to forget just how useful pen and ink are. The simple fact is that many senior businesspeople prefer to write everything out in longhand, as do many novelists and other professional writers. I tend to write first drafts on my word processor, but I revise in longhand on hard copy (ie the print-out), and often my revisions are so extensive they amount to a complete rewriting.

Pen and ink are also ideal if you want to write when travelling. Writing in longhand does not annoy people as tapping the keys of a laptop does, and when you want to stop and take a look out of the train window or watch the movie in the aeroplane's cabin, there's no need to take time to save anything; you just stop.

15

Pen and ink can also provide a pleasant 'hands-on' feeling when you write and give you the sense of being the writer as wordsmith or 'maker' of a written text rather than as a mere manipulator of words. Some people find that this feeling of being a wordsmith helps to improve their writing. And of course, we have to treat with immense respect the writing method that Shakespeare used.

2. The typewriter

The typewriter was invented in order to enable people to write more rapidly – and more legibly – than could be achieved with pen and ink. The typewriter was always first and foremost a business tool: its invention was driven by the needs of nineteenth century commerce for a more rapid writing device. An important advance in typewriting was the invention of the electric typewriter, which is basically a mechanical typewriter with the typing stroke powered by an electric motor.

Typewriters are fast – even someone who types with two fingers can type considerably faster than when writing in longhand – and have the same advantages as pen and ink of instantly putting the words on the page and easily preserving what you have written. The biggest drawbacks of typewriters are that they are too cumbersome to use when travelling, and are noisy.

Generally, typewriters have now been superseded by word processors and other computerised writing tools. However, some writers continue to use them, and everybody who has ever lost text on a word processor because it malfunctioned or because they forgot to save it, will be forcibly aware that this would not have been a problem had they used a typewriter.

Some electric typewriters have an electronic component which allows a small amount of text to be stored in memory prior to being printed out. I must say I have never seen any point in these devices, which occupy a kind of median position between the typewriter and word processor, and which, in any event, are evidently being phased out.

3. The word processor

I use this term to cover any kind of writing tool which involves the text being keyed into a computer memory and displayed on a cathode-ray screen or liquid crystal display prior to being revised and printed out. Whether the computerised aid is a word processor that stands on your desk, or has the portability of a laptop or palmtop machine, the principle is basically the same.

The enormous advantage of word processors, and the reason why they have to a large degree made manual or electric typewriters an obsolete technology in offices, is that they dispense with the laborious need to retype material. The writer can revise text on the screen before printing it, then revise the print-out and limit retyping to any specific changes.

This huge benefit has revolutionised the manipulation of words in offices; it has put people firmly in command of words and has at a stroke removed much of the drudgery which the production of text used to involve.

Word processors also have the subsidiary advantage that they allow any number of copies of a document to be produced, although repeat copies of a document can of course also be made with a photocopier.

So complete has been the word processor's triumph over the

typewriter that purists often resent it. Some highly experienced business writers – in common with some authors – resolutely refuse to use word processors, sticking instead to the typewriter or pen and ink. Making that choice is reasonable enough; what is unreasonable is to be opposed to word processors simply because they are a more recent invention than their predecessors.

One eminent publisher, in a recent edition of a writers' handbook published in the UK, accused writers who use word processors of being over-wordy and careless with their revisions. While I accept that *some* writers who are new to word processors may be tempted, by the sheer ease of correcting, to produce first drafts that are less polished than even the average first draft ought to be, I rather think that before long the user ceases to be conscious of the tool. He or she simply writes with it and enjoys its benefits, not the least of which is that because it makes revision so easy, the word processor can be said positively to encourage revision. Because revision is so crucial to the quality of a piece of writing, this means that in effect the word processor encourages better writing.

17

Nor should the principal drawback of word processors – that it is easy to lose completed text from the memory if you are careless about saving it – be permitted to detract from the advantages these machines offer. All you need to do is get into the habit of saving what you have written every few pages (or even more often, if you are particularly nervous about losing text), and making sure that if you are saving your work onto a floppy disk (i.e. a disk that can be taken out of the machine) you ensure that at all times you have *at least one*, and ideally two, back-up disks with the very latest version of your work on them.

Don't ever neglect the importance of having back-up disks, even if you have complete confidence in your word processor's efficiency at saving material. Unfortunately, floppy disks can spontaneously corrupt, losing text forever no matter how carefully you preserve them from excessive sunlight, magnetic sources and coffee spillages. There have been at least three occasions in my writing career where if I had not had a fully current back-up disk to hand, I would have had to retype close to a fortnight's work.

Note that many word processors – and some laptops and palm-tops – have a built-in hard disk on which you save material and that in some cases the machine will save material *automatically* onto the hard disk. However, you will probably still want to save material onto a floppy disk anyway, in order to have a back-up. Laptop and palmtop hard disks are relatively limited in their memory capacity; you will probably need an auxilliary floppy disk as an additional memory medium.

I strongly recommend that if you have not already obtained access to an efficient word processor, you do so now. Your choice should be between a computer which has a powerful word pro-cessor program but can also be programmed with other types of software to carry out a range of disparate functions (e.g. account-ing, stock-keeping, management information provision etc.), and a dedicated word processor which either has the word processing package built into the hard disk or is designed to use a specific word processing package introduced on a floppy disk.

18

If you decide to choose a multi-function computer, select one which is IBM-compatible. Many word-processing packages – such as Word 6, which can be run with Windows 95 – check spell-ing and provide templates for different types of document. If you choose a dedicated word processor, give consideration to the Amstrad machines, which are inexpensive and reliable, and accessories for which – ribbons, disks and spare parts – are usu-ally readily available. They also provide document templates.

You will find a glare-reduction net placed over your screen an excellent way to minimise or eradicate eye strain. Do not sit hunched over the screen; for maximum visual comfort make sure your eyes are at least two feet or so away from it.

Another hazard of working with a word processor is repetitive strain injury (RSI): a neural condition caused by constant use of a particular finger or fingers to tap a key. I had a bad attack of RSI – which is a demoralising condition for a professional writer – early in 1995, mainly through working ridiculously long hours typing out a lengthy book. I was cured by limiting my daily writing sessions to no more than about six hours, having a short rest every hour or so and using a wristpad: a hard cushion about eighteen inches long, three inches broad and an inch thick, which is placed on the desk in front of the keyboard. Its great virtue is that it gives you a place to rest your wrists while hitting the keys and thereby avoids strain being placed on your wrists, which would otherwise be resting awkwardly against the desk.

So now you are set up with the preliminaries of being a writer. You understand what the point of writing is, you understand the need to be professional in your attitude, to spell your work correctly, to weed out typos, to make your writing appear like the spoken language written down, you are ready with whatever writing tool you have chosen and are raring to go. Before we start looking at specific technical points to which you must pay attention if you are to write marketing copy that gets you ahead in your career, are there are any general rules which you should apply to all your writing?

There are, and I conclude this chapter with them.

General rules for writing well

19

■ ■ ■

1. Keep it brief

Your aim in writing should be to express what you want to say in as few words as you can. In *Hamlet*, Shakespeare has Polonius say that 'brevity is the soul of wit'. This comment – itself a beautiful example of crisp use of language – means that the more concisely and economically you can write (or speak, for that matter), the better your writing, or speech, will be.

The secret of writing concisely and economically is to make the words do the work by choosing the precise ones, rather than choosing ones that aren't quite right and piling them up against one another. I have already shown how the advertising slogan 'Players Please' and the Shakespearian line 'Shall I compare thee to a summer's day?' are messages which achieve their effect precisely because they say what they want to say briefly and without any superfluous use of words. 'Compare' is obviously much more to the point than 'effect a comparison between' and 'summer's day' is clearly much more concise than 'any unspecified twenty-four period occurring at or around the summer solstice'.

Very well, I did indeed choose the latter example partly with the aim of humour in mind. All the same, it amazes me how clumsy and careless people are when they write. Even professional writers are often far too long-winded. Here is a hypothetical, but by no means far-fetched, example of what I mean.

✍ EXAMPLE 3

The new Novon vacuum cleaner is one of the very best vacuum cleaners you can buy with your money. It looks very stylish and the clean lines of its design show that here is an object that is both fashionable and beautiful. Its sucking power really is quite remarkable; it simply loves dirt and dust and goes round your house leaving it in the very best condition possible. Yes, here is a vacuum cleaner for the twenty-first century! The Novon comes complete with a range of cleaning accessories, too, and all for just £129.99.

Let's see whether we can boil this flabby and long-winded piece of writing down to something a good deal punchier. Let's take it sentence by sentence.

The new Novon vacuum cleaner is one of the very best vacuum cleaners you can buy with your money.

Do we need to say it's a vacuum cleaner so soon after we mention its name, when we say what it is later in the sentence?

Why say 'you can buy *with your money*'? How else are you going to buy something? It simply isn't necessary.

It looks very stylish and the clean lines of its design show that here is an object that is both fashionable and beautiful.

Basically most of this sentence is a tautology: that is, an unnecessary repetition of words, phrases or ideas which have already been used. Everything in this sentence after the word 'stylish' is in fact, summed up by 'stylish'.

Its sucking power really is quite remarkable; it simply loves dirt and dust and goes round your house leaving it in the very best condition possible.

When the Americans say that something 'sucks' they mean that it is bad, useless or rubbish and those sentiments can readily be applied to this sentence, even if you don't intend it to be read by Americans. (If you do, you certainly couldn't say *its sucking power really is quite remarkable* without risking some wag choosing to interpret this as your saying that the Novon is useless).

Note also that any phrase involving the words ... *the very best ... possible* or this phrase in conjunction with any other superlative is one of the oldest clichés of business writing. It's a dreadful, lazy expression that simply drips with insincerity. What does it mean, anyway? How can anything tinged with the inevitable flaws of man-made things ever be the very best possible? Why not say something *alive* about the wretched vacuum cleaner?

The sentence also contains an illogicality: something all too common in first drafts of marketing copy. Vacuum cleaners don't go round houses by themselves: not unless they are being driven by a poltergeist, anyway.

Incidentally, *home* is better than *house*, being much more intimate and personal.

21

> *Yes, here is a vacuum cleaner for the twenty-first century!*

This is rather a tired sentiment if presented in such a open-ended, uncorroborated way. What exactly does it mean, *a vacuum cleaner for the twenty-first century*? That you can use it on the moon?

> *The Novon comes complete with a range of cleaning accessories, too, and all for just £129.99.*

Ironically, this last sentence is about the best one in the piece, as it communicates information with the minimum of unnecessary words. Which does not mean there are *no* unnecessary words in the sentence, because there are. I presume you can spot them.

Let's now revise the piece to make it more concise:

> *The new Novon is the best vacuum cleaner you can buy. Stylish, powerful and efficient, it loves dirt and dust, leaving your home beautifully clean and fresh. It comes complete with a wide range of accessories to meet your changing cleaning needs in the future. All this for just £129.99.*

I'm not suggesting this is a masterpiece of marketing copy, but I don't think anyone could reasonably doubt that in reducing the length of the piece of copy by about half, we've made it at least twice as good. Writing is one of the few areas of life where reduction almost always means improvement.

2. Use familiar words

This rule is a direct consequence of the guiding principle that your writing should read like the spoken language.

Unless you are writing legal language (where the overriding objective is not to be interesting but to make your meaning utterly and completely clear), there should be no room in your marketing copy for words which are not used every day, unless of course you use pompous words to create a particular effect.

What this principle means, simply, is that you should only use words which are used in everyday speech.

This point only needs making because many people – even otherwise highly intelligent and resourceful people – make the strange assumption that written language should somehow be more formal, elaborate and consciously 'literary' than spoken language. As a result, they use a completely different kind of language when they write than when they speak.

They're wrong. Why on earth should formal, literary words be better for communicating your written message than the familiar, everyday words you would use if you were speaking?

How do you decide whether or not a word is an everyday word? English is a hybrid language, a mixture of Anglo-Saxon and Norman French, and generally speaking the Norman French words in our language are more formal and stilted than the Anglo-Saxon ones. After William the Conqueror took over Britain he installed his Norman French friends and hangers-on in the castles and mansion houses of the realm, having first kicked out or killed off the Anglo-Saxon lords of the manor. The common people, who did the dirty work, were allowed to go about their business much as before, as long as they didn't step out of line.

The result was that for at least a hundred years the local squires spoke Norman French (the very word squire is a Norman French word) and the serfs and peasants spoke Anglo-Saxon. An illustration of this which has survived in modern English is that generally speaking names of farm animals are Anglo-Saxon words, but change to French words when they are served for dinner. The Anglo-Saxons farmed the animals; the French ate them.

✍ EXAMPLE 4

ANGLO-SAXON	FRENCH
swine	pork
cow	beef
sheep	mutton
calf	veal

A similar process took place with more conceptual words. The Anglo-Saxon would 'see', his French squire would 'regard'. The Anglo-Saxon would 'start' or 'begin', the squire would 'commence'. For clarity, I am using the modern forms of the old words.

23

In due course, as the squires and their friends started to see themselves as British rather than French, the use of Norman French in Britain began to die out. This did not, however, mean that everybody went back to speaking Anglo-Saxon. Instead, a new kind of language evolved – scholars call it Middle English – which was a hybrid containing both Anglo-Saxon and French words. The Anglo-Saxon words tended to be the most succinct, direct, everyday words (as befitted the station in life of the people from whom they originated) and the French words tended to be more elevated and formal, also appropriate to the people from whom they came.

Many of the French counterparts to the Anglo-Saxon words have now died out (for example, there is no French equivalent in modern English of 'drink' or 'think', although we do have the word 'pensive' [French *penser*] as a formal synonym for 'thoughtful'), but sufficient French counterparts remain for there to be two clearly identifiable registers of language in English: the informal and the formal.

✍ **EXAMPLE 5**

INFORMAL	FORMAL
Help me!	Render me assistance!
I want some food	I desire nourishment
I love you	I am amorously inclined towards you

Here, the formal alternatives seem comic because their higher register of language appears ludicrously inappropriate in relation to the simplicity and directness of the informal statement. In many respects it is puzzling why many of the words on the right have survived at all. Take, for example, the word 'desire' used as a verb. Why has the language preserved it? Nobody apart from a gigolo eager to create a good impression would be likely to use it in everyday speech, and about the only written context I can think of where it would be preferable to 'want' would be where a novelist was setting down the speech of that gigolo.

Its survival is probably due to two factors:

a, the survival of the useful noun 'desire' having had the effect of keeping 'desire' around as a verb, too;

b, the fondness which English has for delicate shades of meaning. If you doubt this, buy or borrow a thesaurus and take a look.

As a writer of marketing copy you should certainly concern yourself with delicate shades of meaning, but you should be even more concerned about making your writing direct, vivid and easy to understand. Like all the rules and principles I suggest in this book, there are occasions when this particular rule can beneficially be broken, but generally speaking it holds fast: **use familiar, everyday words, and don't bother with the formal and literary ones**.

3. Use words which refer to clearly identifiable things

Not only should you use familiar, everyday words, but you should as far as possible use words which refer to things that are clearly identifiable and readily understood.

By this I mean things such as objects (e.g. a table, a river, a star, an aeroplane, a fish, a vacuum cleaner) and familiar concepts (e.g. day, night, summer, spring). Words relating to abstract ideas and concepts (e.g. happiness, sorrow, pleasure, delight, thought, beauty) ought to be avoided in your marketing copy unless you have an extremely good reason for including them.

Again, this rule follows from the basic principle that you write in order to communicate a message. Although the precise meaning of a word in terms of the associations and thoughts it conjures up, will never be exactly the same for two different people, words referring to clearly identifiable objects have sufficient number of associations in common for them to be useful as communication tools. The same is true, although not quite to such an extent, of words referring to familiar concepts.

However, words referring to abstract ideas or concepts are less efficient as tools of the communication process, for two reasons.

Firstly, they do not summon up in the reader's mind any immediate image or set of images (as 'table', 'fish', 'night' and 'summer' would do).

Secondly, what they mean to different people is likely to differ widely, with the result that your message is likely to be blurred, or even not communicated at all. For example, I am a keen coarse fisherman, and one of the many images the word 'happiness' summons up for me is sitting by my local lake on a summer's evening and watching my float in the hope that it might register a bite. (I always return the fish to the water). If you, on the other hand, were vehemently anti-angling, your idea of happiness might be to throw a large stone near my float to frighten all the fish away.

Consider also the following two sentences:

✍ **EXAMPLE 6**

Come on a Sunshine Tour to the West Indies and spend your evenings sipping exotic drinks under the shade of a palm tree and chatting to new friends.

Come on a lovely Sunshine Tour to the West Indies and enjoy yourself at our beautiful resorts.

In the second sentence, 'lovely', 'enjoy' and 'beautiful' are all abstract words which in this context sound superficially positive but in fact tell the reader nothing about the experience of going on a Sunshine Tour.

The first sentence, on the other hand, contains several words which refer to particular things: 'evenings', 'drinks', 'shade', 'palm tree', 'friends'. True: 'exotic' and 'new' are abstract words, but because they are used as qualifying adjectives for words whose meaning is clear, they add to the sentence.

Note, too, that apart from the purely linguistic differences between the first and second sentence, the first sentence is far more effective because it *dramatises* and *particularises* the experience of going on a Sunshine Tour, rather than just *telling* you what it will be like. As living, breathing human beings inhabiting a physical world of the senses, **our imaginations and emotions are much more likely to be engaged by the dramatic and the particular rather than the abstract**, and if the dramatic and the particular can be conveyed by powerful sensory information which makes the experience real and vivid to us, so much the better.

26

I return to this crucial point in chapter three, where I look at style.

KEY LEARNING POINTS

- **You cannot be a good writer unless you take writing seriously.**
- **Writing for strangers is more demanding than writing for people who know you.**
- **The aim of writing is to communicate something to your readers.**
- **Ensure your copy is free from spelling, punctuation and typographical errors.**
- **Know and use the rules of grammar.**
- **Good writing is not 'literary': it resembles the spoken language.**
- **Keep your copy brief and to the point.**
- **Stick to specifics and avoid abstract words.**

2
■ ■ ■

Fundamentals: (1) Structure

27

Introduction

■ ■ ■

Speaking well is easier than writing well. We speak at our best – that is, at our most direct, forceful and interesting – when we have urgent messages to convey: requests, commands, wishes, plans, pleas. When we don't, we flounder: we bore people by talking too much about ourselves or about a hobby-horse that fascinates us, we give after-dinner or best-man speeches that send our audience to sleep, we present a dull discourse at a business conference and forget that speaking at a business conference is a performance art best left to the professionals or the experts.

Mostly, though, we have relatively few problems communicating through speech. Easiest of all is talking to *one person* rather than several; we can generally assume that the person we're talking to wants to be there with us. As such, that person is a willing listener: the success of the communication process is already half-assured. If you have ever gone out on a blind date, you will know that if the other person really isn't interested in you or has nothing in common with you, even having a polite conversation about superficialities is difficult. Conversation is something you can only carry out with success when you have some real liking, or at least some sympathy and understanding, for the other person.

Speaking well is also easier than writing well because we have more experience of it. As a species, we were talking for about a quarter of a million years before we began to write. As individuals, we learn to speak at least five years before we start to write with any degree of fluency.

Writing well is something we must learn even if we are fortunate to be born with some talent for writing. As I have suggested earlier, I am convinced there are no short cuts to learning how to write well; it takes experience and practice.

The fruits of experience and practice cannot readily be taught. The ability to choose which word you want, the capacity for discriminating between the infinitely subtle differences of meaning which the thousands of not-quite-synonyms English offers, the ability to twist a simple idea into something verbally expressive and exciting: these are all a part of writing and to a large extent can only be learned the hard way: by working at writing.

On the other hand, just as a musician needs to be able to play scales, arpeggios and all the simple tunes before being able to produce brilliant improvisations, a writer needs to learn the fundamentals of writing before writing brilliant copy.

We can usefully classify this fundamental information into two categories: **structural** and **stylistic**.

In this chapter I look at structure, and in the next consider style.

Why structure is so important

■ ■ ■

The importance of structure in writing is due to two factors:

29

- ■ The need for your writing to communicate efficiently to your reader.
- ■ The strictly limited nature of the written message as a message.

When you speak to someone, what you say is only a part of the communication process. The tone of your voice, the facial and hand gestures you use, even your bodily posture, will also convey meaning. It is quite possible that what you are really saying will not be represented by your words at all. This is particularly the case when two people know each other very well: what they say to each other is often intensely at odds with what they mean. This is why being in the same room as two lovers who are quarrelling can be so disconcerting: they may use harsh language, even curse one another, but such is the level of intimacy they have together that the harshest curses may be their way of expressing a fond affection.

When you write you have no other communication tool except the words. Get the words wrong, and the communication will miscarry.

It follows that to get the words *right* you need to structure them in such a way that the reader will understand what you are saying. The originality of expression and meaning which characterises the best writing is certainly what you should ultimately be aiming for, but you can't strive for originality of expression and meaning at the expense of good structure. The best writing is both original *and* well structured.

Grammar

■ ■ ■

Grammar is the system of rules spoken and written language must obey if it is to sound correct to a native speaker. Grammar is the skeleton of a language, without which nothing works. Like language itself, it is purely a convention based on what is regarded by the community of speakers as acceptable usage.

The point that grammar is merely good, accepted usage needs making, because many of us associate grammar with the formal rules of Latin and see it as something dead, dismal and threatening. (The term 'grammar school' originally referred to a school where Latin grammar was taught).

It is untrue to speak of one language as having 'more grammar' than another. A baby, wherever it is born, will speak as its mother tongue whatever language its mother speaks to it, and children around the world progress in the knowledge of their mother tongue at a remarkably similar rate. The American linguist Noam Chomsky has advanced the widely accepted theory that the similarities in the speed at which children learn their mother tongue is due to all languages having a similar 'deep structure', with superficial differences in how they express ideas being just that: superficial. We do not know how quickly Roman children mastered Latin, but we can safely assume they took no longer to master it than Italian children nowadays take to master Italian.

However, there is no doubt that languages *do* differ in their major areas of grammatical complexity.

Latin, for example, has five noun declensions and four verb conjugations: English has one of each. Latin, and all the modern languages derived from Latin – as well as several modern Germanic languages – feature grammatical gender: that is, words are either male or female (and in some languages neuter, too) and there are complex rules of agreement relating to words which are used in some kind of relation to nouns. The late Anthony Burgess pointed out that grammatical gender, which has terrorised English schoolchildren for hundreds of years, is completely unnecessary, but Burgess was English. To a modern Frenchman or German, getting the grammatical gender of a noun wrong does not usually inhibit comprehension, but it still sounds completely unacceptable, just as it would surely have sounded to a Roman of classical times.

The English noun features no grammatical gender, and the only variable forms are the plural (e.g. tables, typewriters) – the vast majority of which are perfectly regular (apart from a few words like ox/oxen, and child/children, where we retain the Anglo-Saxon plural) – and the possessive (e.g. the table's legs, the typewriter's ribbon).

31

On the other hand, English has extremely rigid rules about word order, which in Latin was evidently fluid. The reason for the difference is the extent to which the two languages enable the function of a word in a sentence to be ascertained from the word. In English, apart from the plural and the possessive cases, you can't work out the role a word is playing in a sentence simply by looking at its ending, whereas in Latin you usually can.

Human language is a product of the communal human intellect, rather than the individual intellect. As such, it is probable that not even the completely fluent native speaker of a language knows all the grammatical rules of that language. This is because grammar ultimately reaches into many areas where what is correct usage is a matter of opinion rather than fact. This being the case, how do you ensure your writing is grammatical?

The only reliable answer to this question is that *you must ensure your writing makes sense and seems correct to you as a speaker of English*.

There are of course many books which aim to put down grammatical rules in factual form, but the truth is that the complexity of grammar means that a full statement of a language's grammatical rules cannot be entirely set down in the form of logical rules. Certainly many rules of grammar *can* be set down, but ultimately exists as a set of perceptions in the mind of a competent speaker of the language.

It is these perceptions that tell you, for example, that 'I placed the typewriter on to the table' is correct and 'I places typewriter along table' is wrong. One reason why teaching English as a foreign language is so difficult is that in many cases the difference between what is acceptable and unacceptable is so narrow there are no obvious rules: as a native speaker you simply know what is right or wrong.

It follows that if you want to write grammatically (which you *must* do, if you are to write well), your most precious asset is your own inbuilt competence as a speaker of English.

I am writing this book for native speakers of English and non-native speakers with a high degree of competence; this isn't the place to try to set down every important rule you need to follow if you are going to write grammatically. Still, it is useful to look at areas which cause particular problems. In what follows I try to identify what seem to me the main problem areas.

Analysis of particular grammatical difficulties in English

■ ■ ■

1. Sentences and phrases

My *Shorter Oxford English Dictionary* defines a sentence **as a series of words in connected speech or writing, forming the grammatically complete expression of a single thought**. Yes, we often use sentences when we speak, but frequently we don't, because the urgency of our message is more important to us than creating an elaborate sentence.

If, for example, you fell into a river and found yourself being swept along to a dangerous weir, you'd be unlikely to call out to someone on the bank *I need a lifebelt, please*. You'd more likely say *A lifebelt, for God's sake*! In fact, analysis of actual conversational speech, even in non life-threatening situations, reveals that not only do we speak with many hesitations and repetitions, but we also do not by any means always form what could be described as a good sentence.

✍ EXAMPLE 7

A lady who is telling her best female friend of her plans to leave her current boyfriend and go off with somebody else would be less likely to say *I'm leaving Jeremy for Mike next week* than something resembling *Jeremy and I ... well, we've been having ... you know, difficulties, problems ... like when we were ... when we were in Stratford, as I told you ... so ... anyway, now Mike's appeared on the scene and I ... well, I just think we're great together ... I've told ... I've told Jeremy. I'm ... I'm moving in with Mike ... yes, I really am ... next week.*

So where does this leave you, as a writer who wants your writing to have the same directness and urgency as the spoken language? Well, what it certainly *doesn't* mean is that you can write as the woman in the above example speaks (and this meandering speech is surprisingly representative of how we convey even the most personal, urgent and sensitive information about ourselves). Instead, in your writing you have to try to *simulate* urgency and directness.

33

One highly effective way of doing this is to use phrases which have some sequential meaning but which do not have the relative formality of sentences. Consider the following example.

✍ EXAMPLE 8

This year, for the first time ever, Sunshine Tours opens its Youthful Frolics holiday village, which is located on a beautiful artificial island a mere thirty minutes by ferry from Kingston, Jamaica. When you stay at Youthful Frolics, you know that everybody you meet on the island – yes, even the staff – will be in the magical age range eighteen to thirty-five, and that your choice of entertainment will be marvellously wide, ranging from the Twenty-Four Hour Rave Party to the numerous restaurants, pubs, discos, shops and also including special attractions such as bungee jumping, ice-skating, gladiators, and scuba diving.

There are just two sentences here. The second is somewhat longer than the first, but has the same classical construction of subject, verb and remaining elements which make up the meaning.

Let's now try to describe this ghastly village in a fashion that the unfortunates who would actually go to such a place might appreciate.

This is the year. This is the year it happens. You asked for it; you got it. Yes, Sunshine Tours has opened its Youthful Frolics holiday village on a beautiful artificial island in the sun-drenched Caribbean. Sounds inaccessible? It isn't. Get yourself to Kingston, Jamaica, and you're just a thirty-minute ferry ride away. And then you arrive, and what an arrival it is. Everyone on the island – yes, even the staff – is in that fun age range eighteen to thirty. It's less a village, more a continuous explosion of delight. You name it, it's there. A twenty-four hour rave party. Restaurants serving mouth-watering cuisine. Pubs. Discos. Shops. Special attractions, too, including bungee jumping, ice-skating, gladiators, and scuba diving.

34

The structure of this version is much less formal than that of the first version, with many of the phrases not constituting sentences at all, but merely brief phrases, and even some one-word phrases. But, it's important to note that even this deliberately 'dynamic' and 'youth-orientated' piece of writing has a relatively formal structure to it, compared with the repetition and hesitation of speech.

The point is that there is no getting away from the principle that writing is a more formal way of communicating than ordinary speech. You *can* get away with short phrases and one-word chunks of meaning when you write, but often the effect of these is somewhat pretentious and impertinent, which is fine if you're writing copy for places like Youthful Frolics, but otherwise rather tends to irritate the reader.

Generally, it's best to err on the side of caution, and use proper sentences unless you're sure that the ambitious effect you're trying to create is going to strike home.

And yes, your teachers were right. Your sentences need a subject and a verb.

2. Getting your sentences the right length

Generally your sentences should not be too long. I realise that this is a somewhat crass generalisation, and no doubt you can think of many examples of good marketing copy in which lengthy sentences feature.

But you are reading this book for practical guidance, and my advice here is to keep your sentences relatively short unless there are good reasons for it.

The main reasons for writing longer sentences are:

- **When you are seeking to gain the effect of a series of features or advantages being heaped up against one another:** this effect can be very powerful. However, frequently the effect is even better if you make your features or advantages into a short phrase as in the second version of the copy about Youthful Frolics, above.

- **When you want your sentence to take the reader through a sequence of meaning that mimics the progression of a series of thoughts:** this is why there are a fair number of lengthy sentences in this book. I have a personal liking for sentences that imitate the path of a train of thought, and I have found them particularly useful as ways to explain the ideas and precepts in this volume.

- **When the rhythm of the sentence is attractive and helps your meaning along:** good writers are essentially musicians, with the music being the creation of prose rhythms. If a lengthy sentence is well crafted, the beauty of its rhythm can give a lovely strength and vigour to the meaning. Consider the first two sentences of Daniel Defoe's masterpiece, *Robinson Crusoe*:

✍ **EXAMPLE 9**

I was born in the year 1632, in the city of York, of a good family, tho' not of that country, my father being a foreigner of Bremen, who settled first at Hull. He got a good estate by merchandise, and leaving off his trade lived afterward at York, from whence he had married my mother, whose relations were named Robinson, a very good family in that country, and from whom I was called Robinson Kreutznaer, but by the usual corruption of words in England, we are now called, nay, we call ourselves and write our name, Crusoe, and so my companions always called me.

Here, the swift rhythm of the sentences not only helps get you into the story quickly but also creates the effect of the writer urgently sharing important confidences with you.

✍ EXAMPLE 10

Here, the eighteenth-century historian Edward Gibbon, describing how he decided to write his great work *The History of The Decline and Fall of the Roman Empire*, uses the long sentence to dramatise the idea of the present inspiring an exhaustive investigation of the past.

It was on the fifteenth of October, 1764, in the gloom of the evening, as I sat musing amidst the ruins of the Capitol, while the bare-footed friars were singing vespers in the Temple of Jupiter, that the idea of writing the decline and fall of the city first started to my mind.

36

But the expert wielding of the long sentence can be as effective in marketing copy as it is in literature, it is not an easy technique to use, and unless you know what you are doing it is horribly easy for your sentence to deteriorate into something dull and slovenly. So, until you are confident you know how to handle a long sentence, it is better to keep your sentences punchy and short.

For example:

The Novon is the best vacuum cleaner you can buy.

Carson Cars announces the launch of the new Stellar family car.

This is a true story.

If you *do* want to use lengthy sentences, you will probably want to divide the sentence into clauses with commas in order to give your reader a breather. If so, you *must* make sure that all the clauses make sense both as units and in the context of the entire sentence.

Above all, when you have written your long sentence, check that it does not read much better if you break it up into two or more shorter sentences. Very often it will. If it does, break it up.

How do you know for certain whether your sentence reads better as a long sentence or as a succession of shorter sentences? There is one simple answer: **read it aloud**.

After all, if you are producing writing which is supposed to have the urgency and vigour of the spoken language, your writing *ought* to sound good when you read it aloud.

However much experience you gain, and however skilled you become, one rule remains infallible: **if in doubt, read it aloud**.

3. Paying attention to meaning

What you write must have meaning, and – unless you are deliberately aiming for an ambiguous effect – only *one* meaning.

Meaning is not something which will take care of itself if the sentence is well constructed and grammatical. Meaning is something you have to work for all the time, a living dynamic that arises from the energy and expressiveness with which you use words. True, if your sentence isn't grammatical your meaning will not be properly conveyed, but don't imagine that grammatical correctness is somehow a substitute for putting every ounce of your passion, energy and determination into the meaning of what you write.

In fact, it is possible for a sentence to be completely grammatical and yet entirely meaningless. The classical example of such a sentence was concocted by the linguist, Noam Chomsky. His sentence was:

Colourless green ideas sleep furiously.

This is grammatically correct in every sense, but means nothing whatsoever. Remember it whenever you are tempted to substitute grammar for meaning.

I can't teach you to make your writing meaningful. This is one of the areas of writing which is an art, and for which you must rely on your intelligence, experience of writing and ability to criticise your own work.

Meaningfulness, however, is ultimately what good writing is all about, and if you can cram great swathes of meaning into a few words, your writing may have a chance of being great. The main reason why Shakespeare's work seems complex is that he compresses meaning so powerfully, economically and succinctly that a single speech (or, indeed, a single line) will have a world of meaning in it. The people who read your marketing copy will not be prepared to make the same effort that we have to make to understand Shakespeare. Even so, your writing should as far as possible compress meaning with all the power, economy and succinctness of which you are capable.

One of the surest signs of inexperienced writers is that their sentences – particularly the longer ones – don't have a clear meaning. A fair amount of the time I devote to purely commercial writing is spent rewriting sprawling and meaning-impoverished material that has been produced by otherwise highly gifted people. Indeed, one reason why some of my clients use me is that often the people who write this stuff are so high up in the organisation that nobody who works for them would dare correct their work.

It wouldn't be fair to quote any real-life examples of the writing I have to rework, but the following is typical of the sort of thing I mean:

✍ EXAMPLE 11

As a bank we make it our task, and an overriding one at that, never to be deficient in areas that good service demands we pay attention to, even if, as is often is the case, there is an upheaval as a result, and re-engineering would be better, as a matter of policy, to undertake.

A sentence as bad as this can't simply be improved by chopping it up into shorter sentences; it needs to be completely recast. The problem here is the problem which features in about 95 percent of bad writing: the writer hasn't worked out what he really wants to say, or if he has doesn't write in a manner that makes logical sense. But perhaps I am being too merciful: maybe the writer is simply too lazy to do the job properly and to read through the work after 'finishing it'.

Again – and this can hardly be over-emphasised – if you are

worried about your ability to create lengthy sentences which have a strong and clearly logical meaning, you can deal with the problem by keeping your sentences short.

Many business people – especially senior ones – imagine that longer sentences are inherently more subtle and profound than shorter ones. I agree that can be, but only if they are constructed with attention to meaning.

However high up you are in the hierarchy of your organisation, if you become an expert at writing marketing copy the day will come when you find yourself staring at a terrible piece of copy which someone even higher up in the hierarchy than you has written (unless you are the boss). That'll be the moment you find out your true strength of character. Do you ask the person what they are really trying to say, or – mindful of the need to pay your mortgage – do you pretend you understand it and pass it on to the printer? Judging by the amount of largely meaningless drivel published in the corporate and product sales literature of the world, most people tend to take the coward's way out.

39

In addition to the hazard of partial or complete meaningless-ness, the other major hazard here is that of ambiguity of mean-ing: where what you write can mean more than one thing. Sometimes the effect can be comical, as:

I know a man with a wooden leg called Harry.

You do? And what was his other leg called?

And certainly there may be occasions when you deliberately want to create an ambiguous effect. This is often seen in adver-tising slogans. *Players Please* is an obvious example.

Mostly, though, ambiguity is a fatal flaw in a piece of writing. Returning to the idea of the message being an arrow, an ambigu-ous sentence is like an arrow that breaks in two as it flies towards its target, with both fragments missing the target com-pletely.

The most common reason for a sentence being ambiguous is that the writer loses track of who or what the subject of the sen-tence – or the subject of a qualifying phrase – is. There isn't any reason why the subject of a fairly lengthy sentence should not change as the sentence progresses, but you must keep precise track of who or what it is, and not permit any ambiguity about this.

A common mistake in this respect would be to write something like:

The Novon is the latest and most advanced product from Innovative Industries, which is a high-powered machine. It sucks like crazy.

Which is the high-powered machine: the vacuum cleaner or the corporation that developed it? And again, this sentence is unlikely to impress customers in America.

Another common error is where the person or object to which a possessive pronoun refers is ambiguous. For example:

The managing director was complaining because the chauffeur had lost his keys.

40

Instead of this, write *The managing director had lost his keys and blamed the chauffeur* or *The chauffeur had lost his keys and the managing director was angry about it* depending on who lost the keys.

Don't, under any circumstances, imagine that ambiguous sentences are acceptable because you get two meanings for the price of one. In fact, you get no meanings for the price of two.

Just as the only way to make sure your sentences have a clear meaning is to take care over composing them and over reading them through once you have written them, the only way to guard against ambiguity is to check your sentences have just one meaning. **Ultimately the meaningfulness and clarity of what you write depends on how much trouble you are prepared to take over your work.** If you feel yourself flagging, or getting tired, or if you simply feel lazy, remember this comment from Oscar Wilde: *talent is the capacity for taking infinite pains.*

Remember, too, that what you write and get printed is going to be around for a long time, maybe for the rest of your life. As you sit sipping your Martini aboard your yacht moored off Nice on a summer evening in 2015, flicking through your portfolio of the work that bought you the yacht, won't you wish you'd taken the trouble to correct that ambiguity which marred an otherwise splendid page?

4. Handling lists

The listing of attributes, features or characteristics can be an extremely powerful technique when writing marketing copy. Not only can the list have an inherent power which comes from the effect of various positive points being piled up one after the other, but there is often scope to put it into a separate and attractive 'box' as a special visual feature on the page.

We saw in the marketing copy for the Youthful Frolics holiday island that one way of setting down a list can be to provide each item as an individual phrase or word. However, generally lists demand a more formal approach.

✍ EXAMPLE 12

> *The new Stellar takes driving into the new millenium. Its space-age features include: autodrive for when you are too busy, too tired or too interested in the view to do the driving yourself, self-sealing, self-inflatory tyres which re-inflate automatically in 1/20th of a second, safety foam shown in tests to prevent injury even in head-on collisions with combined velocities of more than 200 mph., infra-red directional guidance which can be flashed onto the windscreen when you need it, a miniature microwave oven to give you hot snacks whenever you want them, and optional driver-operated release into the air-conditioning of the completely safe, highly effective, patented chemical Cupidin, which increases the susceptibility to seduction of a passenger in the passenger seat by up to 80 percent.*

41

The obvious problem here is that the listing of these features creates a sentence that is much too long and cumbersome. A secondary, related, problem is that because some of the features require qualifying clauses to explain them, there are far too many commas in this example, and the reader will have difficulty knowing what the demarcation points of the individual features actually are.

One way of getting round this difficulty is to use a semi-colon (;) at the demarcation point instead of a comma. This can be an effective technique when the sentence containing the list is relatively short (say, up to about 50 words in total) but where the list is long, as here, it will still leave the sentence unwieldy.

A much better solution in this case, and in cases like it, is to list the features as bullet points, ending each one with a semi-colon, or full-stop, putting a full line between the last one and the next, and introducing each one with a 'bullet', as follows:

The new Stellar takes driving into the new millenium. Its space-age features include:

- *autodrive for when you are too busy, too tired or too interested in the view to do the driving yourself;*

- *self-sealing, self-inflatory tyres which re-inflate automatically in 1/20th of a second;*

- *safety foam shown in tests to prevent injury completely even in head-on collisions with combined velocities of more than 200 mph.;*

- *infra-red directional guidance which can be flashed onto the windscreen when you need it;*

- *a miniature microwave oven to give you hot snacks whenever you want them;*

- *optional driver-operated release into the air-conditioning of the completely safe, highly effective, patented chemical Cupidin, which increases the susceptibility to seduction of a passenger in the passenger seat by up to 80 percent.*

Spelling

■ ■ ■

The only way to master the eccentricities of English spelling is to learn spellings of individual words, one-by-one. As we all discovered at school, there is no way to avoid this.

Dictionaries and word processor spell-check programs certainly help to relieve the burden of having to remember how everything is spelt, and even the best writers often have a few words which they consistently misspell. However, dictionaries and spell-check programs do not represent a complete solution to the problem of spelling your marketing copy correctly. This is because, as in other areas of this complex structure we call language, there are inevitably grey areas where to some extent what is 'correct' is a matter of taste.

Some of the most important of these grey areas are:

1. Use of initial capital letters

This is often poorly understood even by otherwise highly educated and intelligent people, some of whom allocate capital letters rather as if they were writing German (which capitalises *all* nouns). The following is typical of the kind of thing one often sees even in final, printed versions of marketing copy.

✍ EXAMPLE 13

> *Ever since the Information Technology revolution of the late 1980s, occasioned by the use of Personal Computers and the Microchip, our Company, from the Managing Director down to the man in the mailroom, has been striving for a constant policy of Excellence.*

43

There really is no excuse for this kind of erratic and haphazard capitalisation, yet it is alarmingly common.

In fact, English has relatively straightforward rules about capitalisation. You should only use a capital letter if:

- It is the first letter of **the first word of a new sentence**.
- It is the first letter of **the name of a person, an animal or a thing**.
- It is the first letter of **a proper noun**.

This last area is the one that causes the most difficulty, because the definition of a proper noun is less rigid than many people imagine.

The best way of looking at it is to see a proper noun as one used to denote something which is both clearly identifiable as a specific, individual entity and which also has some formality attached to it. If this sounds a fairly woolly definition, this only reflects the principle that the concept of a proper noun is a fairly woolly concept. However, the idea of the thing being specific, individual *and* formal is often extremely helpful when deciding whether or not a noun is a proper noun.

For example, when the word 'government' is being used in a general sense, it should not be capitalised, but when it is used in a specific sense (e.g. the British Government) its formality means capitalising it would be reasonable, although 'the British government' is also a viable alternative. (Note that the *Financial Times* never capitalises the word 'government' unless it is used at the start of a sentence).

My recommendation is that you should *avoid* initial capitalisation unless you are absolutely certain it is correct. Incidentally, under no circumstances capitalise the initial letters of job titles, which always looks dreadful. I realise many organisations do, but there is absolutely no justification for following suit unless, of course, the job title is appearing somewhere on its own, such as on a card or on a door. The *Financial Times* does *not* capitalise the initial letters of job titles unless, as before, the first word of the title is appearing at the start of a sentence.

Some words cause particular difficulty here. The following is a guide to what will most likely be regarded as correct.

Initial capitalisation required:

- Christmas
- Easter
- January (and all the other months)
- Monday (and the other days of the week)
- names of people, animals and things (e.g. Henry, Fido, The Titanic)
- all words which, as mentioned above, denote something identifiable as a specific, individual entity and have some formality attached to them. e.g. the Big Bang, the London Stock Exchange, the Second World War, the Royal Family, the Holocaust etc.

Initial capitalisation not required:

- autumn, winter, spring, summer
- job titles

- all nouns which are not obviously proper nouns. Note that this includes terms which *do* have a certain weightiness, but where the term does not refer to a specific one (e.g. there is only one Christmas) but rather to a general concept e.g. information technology, microchip, personal computer.

2. Writing down brand names

The only reason the writing of brand names causes problems is that too many people who write marketing copy are overawed by them.

The correct form is really very simple:

Start the brand name with a capital letter and put the rest of it in lower-case letters.

This applies even if your sales department insists on spelling the brand name in memos with full capitalisation. Sometimes they go even further and spell it with full capitalisation *and* a little superscript saying 'TM' for trade mark. Resist the temptation to follow suit; your work will look ludicrous and amateurish.

So, instead of writing:

The new NOVON and its sister product, the MINI-NOVON, represent the state-of-the-art in domestic dust extraction

write, simply:

The new Novon and its sister product, the Mini-Novon, represent the state-of-the-art in domestic dust extraction.

If your sales director tells you that either the brand names appear in capitals with 'TM' in superscript or you can look for another job, show him a copy of the *Financial Times*, which *never* spells brand names with capital letters in its editorial pages.

Of course, feel free to use capitals for the brand name in headings and in advertising straplines: I'm just making the point that avoiding full capitalisation looks better when you are writing the main text (often known in the marketing world as the 'body copy').

Incidentally, what is true of brand names is also true of names of organisations that usually appear in capitals: you should restrict the capitalisation in the body copy to the initial letter of the word. The only exception is where the name is obviously an acronym: in this case use full capitalisation *without full stops*.

So, for example, you should write:

> *Many ATM terminals operating on the Link system now accept Visa cards*

even though LINK and VISA are normally written with capitals in these organisations' advertisements.

But you should write:

> *SWIFT is nowadays the major interbank payment system*

as SWIFT is an acronym (Society for Worldwide Interbank Funds Telecommunication). If you are unsure whether a word is an acronym or not, it is safest to assume it is.

3. Putting -ing on the end of certain verbs

We have already seen that the English language – like other languages – has areas where what is 'correct' is to some degree a matter of taste. One such area is, for some words, the decision relating to whether or not to double the consonant at the end of certain verbs before putting an -ing at the end.

This problem does not arise with short, familiar words because the way in which they form the -ing ending is well known. However, some less well known words do present this problem. Everyone knows that the -ing form of transmit is *transmitting*, but do you write, for example, *benefiting* or *benefitting*, *focusing* or *focussing*?

In the case of many words like these, both forms are acceptable. However, my advice is to use the form which *avoids* the consonantal doubling, unless this obviously looks wrong.

4. The decision whether or not to use a hyphen

The hyphen (-) is often, but not always, used where two or more words are linked together in a regularly used combination.

46

For practical purposes, there are three spelling options where words are used in such a combination. These options are:

- Join the words together without a space.
- Join the words together with a hyphen.
- Don't join the words together (i.e. write them with a space in between).

Historically, many words now written together as one word used to be written separately or with a hyphen. For example, Jane Austen wrote 'today' as 'to-day' and tomorrow as 'to-morrow'.

Nowadays, the tendency is to use a hyphen unless writing the words together has become widely accepted.

The use of a hyphen is particularly necessary in combinations which use 'well' or a number, such as:

- well-read
- well-known
- six-month
- five-year
- ten-year.

47

However, there are many words (particularly coined, technological ones) where the decision whether to use a hyphen or join them together is still a matter of taste. e.g.

- nonetheless/none-the-less
- laptop computer/lap-top computer
- palmtop computer/palm-top computer
- layby/lay-by
- jetliner/jet-liner
- microchip/micro-chip

In these cases where both options are acceptable, you should use the joined-up form, unless you you feel it will be found precious or even pretentious by the reader.

Note, too, that there is often the choice between writing the words separately and using a hyphen: e.g.

- first class/first-class
- second class/second-class
- third class/third-class
- front office/front-office
- back office/back-office
- state of the art/state-of-the-art

I must admit that where, as here, there is clear choice between writing the words separately and using a hyphen, I tend to think that writing the words separately looks better, but that is only my opinion. I do break my own rule in one respect: I prefer 'state-of-the-art' to have hyphens.

5. The use of the apostrophe

48

The apostrophe (') is used to show that a letter has been elided. For example:

He isn't coming today, and she's not, either.

where *isn't* is the shorter form of *is not,* and *she's* is the shorter form of *she is* (by the way, a mistake some people make is to write *is'nt* for *isn't*: don't do it).

An even more common mistake here is to confuse *it's* (the elided form of *it is*) with *its*, (the possessive case of *it*). This is probably one of the most common spelling mistakes in English: I've often seen it in printed marketing copy and even in national newspapers. An example of the correct usage of each is:

The Novon's power and reliability, and its superb design, mean it's the best vacuum cleaner you can buy.

The simple rule here is that if *its* is not obviously short for *it is,* don't use an apostrophe. I present the rule this way round because people usually write *it's* when they should write *its*: they think that the *'s* denotes a possessive, which it doesn't.

The apostrophe *is* of course used for the possessive form of nouns, where it replaces an 'e' that was used until around the year 1500.

When the noun is singular the spelling is well-known and rarely causes confusion, e.g.

- the car's engine
- the marketing director's report.

The second example is a floating possessive: the possessive that can be applied to the end of what can be an entire noun-phrase, e.g.

- the Queen of England's corgi
- the young man from Japan's poetry.

Normally, where the noun is plural the apostrophe must be put *after* the 's' rather than before it, e.g.

- the cars' engines
- the marketing directors' conference
- the Factories' Act

but note that the few English words which retain the Anglo-Saxon plural form require the apostrophe to be put *before* the 's'.

49

- the children's toys
- the oxen's carts
- the brethren's habits.

Punctuation

■ ■ ■

I never understand why so many writers regard punctuation as boring and pay insufficient attention to getting it right.

The proper use of punctuation, like the proper use of words, is both an art and a science: that is, there are some areas where what is right or wrong can be assessed with mathematical precision, and others where you must make your own decisions.

I have tried to reflect the art and science aspects of punctuation in the following comments on different punctuation marks.

The full stop (.)

The principal use of the full stop is to show that a sentence has ended. Assuming the sentence isn't the last one of a particular piece of writing, the full stop should always be followed by a capital letter.

The only points of difficulty relating to the full stop are where to place it if the sentence ends with a parenthesis (... .) or [... .], or with an inverted comma (' or ").

The rule is that the full stop should always come *after* the parenthesis, always and *after* the inverted comma when the quotation forms part of a longer sentence, but *before* the inverted comma when the quotation is a complete sentence.

For example:

(Like all our vacuum cleaners, the Novon comes with a five-year guarantee).

and

Some people call the Novon the 'miracle cleaner'.

but

Robert Baker, the managing director of Farmfresh Manure Limited, said, 'This price war must cease. It's bad for our customers, bad for the industry, and bad for manure.'

The full stop is also used to show that a word or term has been abbreviated. However, unless the abbreviation is an extremely well-known one, it is usually better – and also better from the point of view of clarity – to avoid it and write the word or term out in full, instead. What this boils down to is that you can use the following abbreviations, but ought to be wary of using any others.

ABBREVIATION	MEANING
e.g.	for example
etc.	etcetera (and others)
i.e.	that is (Latin *id est*)
viz.	namely

Be careful to avoid confusing 'e.g.' and 'i.e.'. They are sometimes mistakenly used interchangeably, which tends to spoil the sense of the writing.

Note that an acronym (e.g. UK for United Kingdom, IBM for International Business Machines, LSE for London Stock Exchange) is not the same as an abbreviation, and does not require a full stop after it. Full stops after each letter are not necessary, but if your employer or client insists on it, don't lose your job or your account over what is an optional matter.

51

The comma (,)

Proper use of the comma is essential for readability.

The difficulty the comma appears to cause to so many inexperienced and experienced writers is all the more surprising, as there is a foolproof rule for using it properly. This rule is:

Use the comma to mark places where you would want to pause and/or take a breath, if you were reading the text aloud.

There is no mystery about why this rule works. We have already seen how writing is most effective when it has the feel and sound of the spoken language. The comma's role is ultimately not so much to break up sentences, as to make them read well and sound good.

So if you are uncertain where to put a comma, simply **read out your sentence aloud** and make a note of where you want to pause and/or take a breath.

Should you use a comma before 'and'? I only raise this issue because many of us (including myself) were taught at school that you should avoid the use of a comma before the word 'and'.

When you are listing items this advice makes sense. For example:

Our company heads the UK domestic appliance industry, with a leading share of the market in the manufacture and sale of microwave ovens, refrigerators, toasters, electric kettles and bread-making machines.

Here, a comma before 'and bread-making machines' would certainly be redundant, because when you read the sentence aloud you don't need a pause or a breath there.

The trouble with the rule about not using a comma before 'and' is that many people imagine it means you shouldn't *ever* use a comma before 'and', and this is nonsense. Feel free to use a comma before 'and' where, as in the last sentence just now, the 'and' starts a new clause.

What you *must* avoid is the habit, seen in many pieces of published marketing copy, of using a comma simply because there have been a fair number of words since the last one and it seems about time to put one in. Instead, stick to the principle of using a comma where you would pause and/or take a breath while reading the piece aloud, and you will be all right.

This principle is particularly useful for relatively long, complex sentences, which would otherwise be difficult to punctuate properly. For example:

✍ EXAMPLE 14

Here is the first sentence of an article I wrote under a client's by-line about the future of payment technology. First I give it in its unpunctuated form. Where should the commas go?

Predicting the future is never easy but by extrapolating certain present-day trends in retail payment technology it is possible to gain a good idea of how goods will be paid for in the year 2005 and what consumer attitudes towards payment methods are likely to be.

By following my principle, the allocation of commas in this sentence is really quite easy:

Predicting the future is never easy, but by extrapolating certain present-day trends in retail payment technology, it is possible to gain a good idea of how goods will be paid for in the year 2005, and what consumer attitudes towards payment methods are likely to be.

Obviously, your aim should be to get into the habit of knowing instinctively where a comma is required, and inserting it as you are writing the copy. However, even when you have developed this facility, you will still find the principle useful, when you check over your work, as a way of making sure the commas are in the correct places.

The colon (:)

There is little rigidity in the rules of usage of the colon and semi-colon; to a large extent you are free to use them as you wish, given that you understand their primary function, which is to create a sense of an ending in a sentence which is not, however, as final as that which would be created by the full stop.

In the past, this was the principal use of the colon; nowadays there is an increasing tendency for the semi-colon to be used in this way, too.

In my own work, I tend to use the colon only in four areas:

1. To provide a clear, but not final, break in a sentence. Often I will use a semi-colon here, but would use a colon where a semi-colon does not seem quite strong enough.

2. Where I want to introduce a spoken quotation with some impact, and the comma seems too weak for the purpose.

3. Where I want to introduce a list of bullet points.

4. Where I want to introduce something that is italicised or otherwise separated in some sense from the preceding material.

The semi-colon (;)

I must admit that the semi-colon is my favourite punctuation mark. If your writing is to be like fine cookery, you might regard the semi-colon as the garlic. Properly used, it can give your sentence an excitement, a sense of suspense and a sharp flavour that can make the reader as addicted to your work as you can become to your semi-colon.

You can use just one semi-colon if you like, this can often be used to build the sentence up to a kind of peak before you descend to the full stop. For example:

> *Farmers who buy Farmfresh Manure know what to expect; faster growth, healthier crops, higher profits.*

Notice how this sentence has a tension and suspense which would be completely absent if you wrote 'Farmers who buy Farmfresh Manure know what to expect. They can expect faster growth, healthier crops, higher profits.'

Note that the colon could also be used here: whether you use the colon or the semi-colon in this example is a matter of taste.

The full resources of the semi-colon are seen when you want to create several such 'peaks' in your sentence; building up the tension into an argument or statement that appears unanswerable.

This was the effect I tried for (whether or not I succeeded is not for me to say) in a passage from my other book in this series: *Starting a High-Income Consultancy*.

✍ EXAMPLE 15

> *Finally, six months or so after starting out, the secretary leaves when her last salary cheque bounces; the telephone service is cut off due to non-payment; the office equipment (most of which has been obtained on expensive leasing arrangements) is repossessed; and the landlord, whose rent has not been paid for two months, changes the locks on the doors and exercises his right to recover the premises.*

Of course, one way of looking at these different consequences of running an unsuccessful consultancy is to see them as another kind of list; but you should note that here the effect of the clauses which appear within the semi-colons should be to create a cumulative sense of build-up, rather than a mere succession of attributes.

You should also, as we have seen, use the semi-colon or full-stop, at the end of a list of bullet-points, which will of course be introduced with a colon and ended with a full stop.

The dash (–)

The dash is my second favourite punctuation mark. It is extremely useful, and unjustly neglected by many writers.

The beauty of it is that it can give a parenthetical clause a sense of tension and dynamism, without resorting to brackets.

Like bracketed parentheses, the dash needs to be opened and closed, so you need two of them. You should use the dash when you need to make a subsidiary point, but where using round or square brackets would seem pedantic and cumbersome.

✍ **EXAMPLE 16**

55

> *The photo shows John Smith – managing director of Smith International Industries plc – congratulating Edna Jones on her retirement after fifteen years as the company's industrial espionage officer. Mr Smith said: 'Edna's career – which has involved working in twenty-four countries, often undercover – has been a catalogue of lies, deceit and deception. We are proud to have had the privilege of working with her.'*

Note how the dashes allow this passage to retain a flow and dynamism which would be lost if the more formal bracket parentheses were used.

You could also use a comma, or even a semi-colon, where I have used a dash, but I tend to think the dash looks better and gives the sentence a real bite.

Bracket parentheses (...) and [...]

Unquestionably one of the signs of an inexperienced writer is an over-use of bracket parentheses. These are far too often used when what is really required is a semi-colon or a dash.

The trouble with brackets is that they stop the flow of a sentence to such a great extent that it is questionable whether they really belong in good marketing copy at all, except where they are being used to introduce an acronym. Where you are using them for this purpose, the correct form to follow is to write the name – or whatever the acronym refers to – out in full first time round, set the acronym after it in curved brackets, and thereafter use the acronym on its own. For example:

> *The London Stock Exchange (LSE) has today moved to five-day rolling settlement. A spokesman for the LSE said that this was a revolutionary development.*

Brackets are often completely unnecessary, as in this example:

> *Novon vacuum cleaners come complete with full accessories and a five-year guarantee. (Note, however, that an additional charge of £29.99 is made for the full ten-year guarantee).*

The brackets give the erroneous impression that the material they enclose is unrelated to the preceding sentence. In fact, it is related to the section. They can be left out.

On rare occasions you may need to use a hierarchy of brackets. Where this is unavoidable use the curved brackets to enclose the square brackets, as in:

> *All models produced in the Worthing factory (that is, models 18–28 [except 23 and 24]) are cold-forged.*

But avoid doing this too often. As you can see, it looks fairly gruesome.

Inverted commas (' and ")

These are used for two main purposes:

1. To indicate that somebody is speaking or that somebody is being quoted.
2. To emphasise that a word or term is being mentioned in such a way as to draw a special attention to it.

There are two kinds of inverted comma: the single inverted comma (') and the double inverted comma ("). Which one you choose is up to you, but remember that where you are quoting additional material *within* the particular type of inverted commas you choose, the additional material quoted must be put inside whichever type of inverted comma is not your main choice. This is necessary to avoid confusing the reader.

For example:

> *Addressing the meeting at the corporation's headquarters in Detroit, vice-president Dick Jones said: 'I have reviewed Bob Morton's "Robocop" proposal and am firmly of the opinion that my own "Enforcement Droid" recommendation is far more likely to prove practically workable and cost-effective.'*

Generally speaking, the tendency nowadays is for the single inverted comma to be preferred as the main one of the hierarchy, but different organisations – or, if you are writing directly for a publisher, different publishers – differ in their approach to this. If you are not pioneering a standard of use of inverted commas, you will probably have to follow an accepted format.

Appendix: the use of italics

57

Italics are not punctuation marks, but as they relate to the way in which your writing is presented on the page they can usefully be considered here.

Italics offer four main potential effects in a piece of writing.

1. Emphasis of a word, phrase or sentence.

2. A useful alternative to inverted commas when you want to quote the name of a work of art such as a film, a book or so on.

3. The opportunity clearly to distinguish between different kinds of writing.

4. They should also always be used when you are using words from another language which are not definitely part of English.

My comments on these different uses are as follows:

1. Using italics for emphasis can be useful and effective, but   to make an emphasis myself – you must be careful to ensure it is the *words* which do the work and that the italics are, so to speak, the icing on the cake. Do not expect, or hope, that the use of italics here and there will somehow turn weak, lifeless writing into strong, vigorous writing.

The sort of thing you must avoid is:

Our company's results over the past year show that we are doing *very* well and are set for a *successful* and *prosperous* future.

This is basically a dull sentence, and the italics don't make it any better. Try again, dump the italics, and aim to show the company's success by referring to a specific example where it has done well, rather than by baldly stating it.

Generally, my advice is to avoid using italics for emphasis at all until you are happy enough with the fluency of your writing to feel ready to emphasise a particular word now and again.

2. Using italics to emphasise the name of a film, a book and other creative works usually looks more professional than using single or double inverted commas.

3. Italics are often useful when you want to distinguish between different kinds of text. Often you can put the italicised passage in a separate box, to give it even greater emphasis.

I have used italics throughout this book to distinguish between my discursive text and my examples. Ironically, the one example which I haven't italicised is the last one above, as italicising all of it would have negated the point of quoting it.

4. You need to use italics when you are quoting words in a foreign language which are not (or, not yet) part of English. However, since the primary aim of writing marketing copy is to communicate an exciting message to readers in a rivetting manner, you ought to give serious consideration to whether you want to use words only a minority of your readers may understand.

KEY LEARNING POINTS

- There are no short cuts to writing well.

- If the structure doesn't work, the meaning will be lost.

- Keep your sentences short.

- Read your writing aloud.

- Avoid ambiguity.

- Use bullet points to make lists effective.

- Do not use initial capital letters unless you are certain they are required. Do not write brand names in capital letters.

- Punctuation is an art and a science. Make it work for you.

3

■ ■ ■

Fundamentals: (2) Style

Introduction

■ ■ ■

M any writers worry about their style, when what they should really be concerned about is expressing their ideas clearly and unambiguously.

But surely style is an essential element of writing? Surely it is foolhardy to deny this?

I agree: style *is* an essential element of writing, which is why it deserves a chapter to itself. But perceiving another writer's style and developing your own style are two very different things.

Moving for a moment from the world of commerce to the world of literature, it is obvious the writers we most admire have their own distinctive style. Consider the following first paragraph of one of the best-loved books in English:

> *My father's family name being Pirrip, and my Christian name Philip, my infant tongue could make of both names nothing longer or more explicit than Pip. So I called myself Pip, and came to be called Pip.*

Even if you have never read *Great Expectations*, this paragraph's the quality of what might be described as energetic long-windedness is likely to lead you to suspect it belongs to the nineteenth century rather than the twentieth. It isn't a lengthy leap from that supposition to conclude that this is probably something by Dickens.

If you or I were writing that paragraph, we'd probably say something like:

> *Call me Pip, everybody else does. I've always had problems saying Philip Pirrip, and I'm sure I'm not the only one.*

We've compressed what Dickens says in thirty-seven words into just twenty-one, although our version has little of the elegance of Dickens's.

When Dickens sat down to write *Great Expectations*, he wouldn't have said to himself, 'I want to say to my readers in this first paragraph that my imaginary narrator is called Pip because he could never pronounce his real name. How can I say that in as long-winded a way as possible?'

No, he just wrote as well as he could. He came from a culture where people spent a long time reading and writing books: detail of expression was believed to go hand-in-hand with subtlety of thought. While Dickens is certainly more than capable of writing fast-moving action sequences when he wants to, his style is generally fairly convoluted and complex, although if either you or I could be half the master of the long sentence that he is, we'd be laughing.

We can discuss Dickens's style as readers, but this book is for writers, not readers, and I emphasise again that Dickens did not set out to create a certain style, but rather to express his thoughts on paper as dramatically and clearly as he could. Had he done anything differently, his writing wouldn't have worked.

63

And what is true of all famous writers is also true of you. Try consciously to write in a particular way and you're doomed to failure. Forget about the style you are trying to cultivate, and instead **write as clearly and concisely as you can**.

If you do that, your style will still be your own. If you are sincere about trying to say what you want to say as effectively as you can, your style will be as individual to you as your fingerprints, and equally impossible for anyone else to copy.

John Braine, author of the bestselling 1950s novel *Room at the Top*, says in a passage in his book *Writing a Novel* everything you need to know about style. Writing of his early efforts to teach himself to write by emulating his favourite writers, he remarks:

> I had the dim idea of creating something out of Hemingway, Joyce, Lawrence and Dos Passos; I even used to copy out passages from them, to imagine myself in their shoes, have some of their talent rub off on me. I realised ... this was adolescent and egoistic. *The function of prose is to convey meaning to as many readers as possible. Style, in the sense of being unmistakably oneself, is a by-product.* The more one consciously strives for it, the further away one will go from it.' (my italics).

I don't know why the style of one writer can differ so greatly from that of another: why, for example, Hemingway's clipped prose and short sentences are such a contrast to the endlessly qualified, meandering sentences of Henry James. But I do know that both these writers have won millions of admirers around the world, and since their styles differ so radically, it *must* be the case there is not really such a thing as a good or bad style, but only a good (or bad) way of expressing what you want to say.

Can we also talk of the style of a piece of marketing copy? Of course we can. The commercial need to grab the attention of a probably indifferent readership militates against writing material that is anything but stunning all the way through, and this will generally require a kind of prose that tends to use shorter sentences rather than longer ones. Yet sentence length is nowhere near as important as the sheer interest which your marketing copy can generate. To maximise a reader's interest in your work, you must use every ounce of the intelligence, resourcefulness, energy and technical ability you possess. Do that, and you will find that your style of writing marketing copy is in every sense as personal and individual as that of any great novelist who ever lived.

There isn't a magic formula for expressing what you want to say as clearly as you can. In previous chapters I have offered specific guidance on the general way you should write, the type of words you should choose, and the attention to detail you should pay to your work, but I can't teach you in any general sense how to express yourself clearly, because in the final analysis your ability to express something in writing is a function of your personality and flair.

What I *can* do is give you guidance on specific areas of expression. I divide this into two areas: *conceptual guidance*, which covers conceptual approaches that make writing more effective, and *textual guidance*, which covers the use (or avoidance) of specific words and phrases.

Conceptual guidance

■ ■ ■

1. Show, don't tell

One of the first lessons any aspiring novelist has to learn is the need to *dramatise* character and events on the page so that these spring up at the reader like the living thing a novel should be, and not simply to *tell* the reader how something is.

For example, if we were to say of the Toad in *The Wind in the Willows* 'he was an irresponsible animal who was indifferent to the feelings of others', that is just a sequence of flat, lifeless words and as dull as pondwater. Now see how Kenneth Grahame makes you *feel* the Toad's irresponsibility and indifference to lesser mortals.

Here, the Toad, who is disguised as a washerwoman, has been given a lift in a motor-car and has been unwisely permitted to sit in the driver's seat.

65

> The driver tried to interfere, but he [the Toad] pinned him down in his seat with one elbow, and put on full speed. The rush of air in his face, the hum of the engine, and the light jump of the car beneath him intoxicated his weak brain. 'Washerwoman, indeed!' he shouted recklessly. 'Ho, ho! I am the Toad, the motor-car snatcher, the prison-breaker, the Toad who always escapes! Sit still, and you shall know what driving really is, for you are in the hands of the famous, the skilful, the entirely fearless Toad!'

It is this energy and drama which explains why every other children's book published in 1908 is long-forgotten, but *The Wind in the Willows* is not only still in print, but has achieved the exalted position of being on sale in supermarkets.

You can strive to inject energy and drama into your marketing copy, too.

The most obvious opportunity to do this is where you are writing copy for a television or print advertisement. In many respects advertising copywriting is all about taking what is on the face of it a dull, and quite possibly untrue, idea – such as the notion that one particular brand of something stands out from the others – and bringing that idea to life. Using chimpanzees to advertise tea; little cartoon men to emphasise the fineness of flour by dramatising their strenuous grading of it; a burly but well-loved actor to generate telephone calls by reminding us that 'it's good to talk'; are just three examples from an industry that never ceases to show great resourcefulness in making the ordinary extraordinary.

Of course, in most marketing copywriting you will probably not have the resources or budget of a large, high-profile consumer products company. Don't imagine this means you should for one moment acquiesce in a situation where your marketing copy is flat and lifeless. Instead, take every step to bring it alive – at least within the constraints of what your organisation or client is prepared to accept.

In my experience, the most useful techniques for bringing copy alive are as follows:

a) The specific dramatic example

Here, just as Kenneth Grahame does in *The Wind in the Willows*, you use a specific dramatic example to drive your point home.

✎ EXAMPLE 17

Imagine you are writing a short sales leaflet for Farmfresh Manure. Your job is to make what is an obviously unglamorous product attractive to cynical farmers who are, perhaps, constantly being bombarded with literature promoting manure.

You could say: 'Farmfresh Manure is the best you can buy. Its freshness, nutrition content and growth enhancement qualities are famous throughout the industry.'

This is a dull and unimaginative solution. Not only is it a typical example of a bland statement that *tells* rather than *shows*, but it makes the cardinal error of focusing on what is, after all, an unattractive product, rather than on the *benefits* of the product.

Do you think the farmer really cares about the manure itself? Of course he doesn't. The days when farmers strode about their land in Wellington boots and thick country clothing, uttering harsh rural gutturals and picking up potatoes to test them for firmness, may not be entirely over, but are fading fast. Nowadays farmers are more likely to spend much of their time in their offices, feeding data and accounting information into a personal computer.

So rewrite your copy for this farmer, making sure you use your imagination to put yourself in the farmer's shoes – or boots. Indeed, you could even use your perception of the traditional role of the farmer as a dynamic element in your copy.

You might come up with something like this:

> *Imagine walking through a field of golden wheat whose every ear is ripe and bursting with goodness. Imagine standing by a stile and seeing your sun-ripened barley stretching to the horizon. Imagine walking back to your office and inputting harvest and revenue forecasts which bring a glow to your heart. Imagine all this, and spare a thought on this day of glorious triumph for Farmfresh Manure, which helped to make it possible.*

67

By particularising and dramatising your message, you make it interesting, absorbing and convincing. A farmer can't readily relate to the nutritional qualities of manure as an abstract concept, but he can easily relate to images of himself walking through a field of golden wheat or seeing his sun-ripened barley stretching to the horizon.

As human beings with a speculative mind, we are certainly able to deal in abstract concepts, but we are essentially animals who are more connected to the earthy realities of life than to the life of the mind. How interested are we in abstract thought when we are extremely hungry? And what would you rather do: read a history of romantic love throughout the ages or watch the person you love take off their clothes and reach out their arms for you?

This lesson, that what fascinates and energises us is the dramatic and specific rather than the abstract and general carries with it another, closely-related, lesson: *know your readers*.

You can't possibly expect to win over your readers unless you know what makes them tick, their main interests, their fears and hopes. If you don't know these things, I suggest you find out before you put pen to paper or finger to keyboard. Get to know your readers' self-interest, do your utmost to imagine them reading your work and try to guess what they will expect of it. Do this, and you're on your way to writing marketing copy that will lodge in the mind for a long time, perhaps for ever.

b) The exciting image

Often your marketing copy assignment will provide ample opportunity to dramatise what you want to say rather than just say it, but this won't invariably be the case. Sometimes you will have to write about a product or set of concepts that simply do not offer any obvious opportunity for drama.

Where this is so, don't despair. Use your imagination to think of images that dramatise your point without your needing to create an entire dramatic framework.

But it must be an *original* image, and an *appropriate* one. Your reader deserves no less.

The use of a powerful image is effective in all kinds of prose, from sales and corporate literature to semi-technical or highly technical articles.

68

✍ EXAMPLE 18

Early in 1995, I was asked by a bank to write an article about the relationship between institutional investors (i.e. the insurance and pensions organisations which invest substantial funds accruing from policy-holders' premiums) and custodians: banks which handle the safe custody and administration of investors' assets. The article had to tease out the difference between global and domestic custody: that is, custody of assets worldwide and in the country where the investor is located. It was a fairly abstruse subject, and I badly felt it needed a sharp image at the beginning to bring the subject-matter alive.

The first sentence I wrote was:

> *For an institutional investor, handling your own domestic cus-tody is like cutting your own hair: it'll probably be cheap to do but the results can be disastrous.*

This is not a particularly brilliant image but it is an intriguing one because, while appropriate for the idea it is supposed to convey, it is at odds with the world of investment. It is sufficiently striking to make the reader want to read on.

I often find that where I want to use an image to drive home a message, it is especially effective to start the piece of writing with it and to conclude the piece with it. This helps to make the whole piece appear a unity and coherent.

Incidentally, it is a mistake to imagine that people with technical knowledge of what you are writing about will not appreciate a dramatic image: they will. Technically-minded people, like writers, are only human.

✍ EXAMPLE 19

When I wrote a highly technical article about an electronic trading system called Globex, I deliberately chose to use a familiar and dramatic image in the first paragraph in order to make an abstruse, difficult subject readily comprehensible. My article began:

> *Assessing a new form of trading technology is like deciding how to bring up one's children. Should we be strict parents who tolerate no nonsense, or should we be genial, indulgent and accept we must make allowances for our offsprings' childish follies?*

And I ended the article with a reference to this same image.

> *In other words, despite the serious reservations about Globex as it stood at the end of March 1994, the system must not be written off. Our children may go through bad phases, but if they are nurtured through these phases and their behaviour modified, why should they not become thoughtful adults who are a real asset to society?*

The use of a dramatic image is another way to show rather than tell: in other words, to make your writing come alive.

2. Use detail in a dynamic way

My next major area of conceptual guidance on maximising the expressiveness of your writing is the dynamic use of detail.

What this means is you should use detail to drive home a point,

69

illustrate a principle, and bring alive what would otherwise be a flat factual statement.

In many respects this dynamic use of detail is closely related to the concept of showing rather than telling, but is so important it deserves a section all of its own.

As human beings who live in the world of the senses we have an inherent fascination with the details of processes, and with the way in which things work. This fascination stems from the huge importance the building of tools has played in our evolution: we first had to create tools in order to survive, then in order to master the world, and now we create tools in order to make our lives as pleasant as we can and to make our leisure time fulfilling and exciting.

I have already mentioned that I am a keen angler: if this is not a pursuit with which you are familiar, I guarantee I could astonish you by taking you to my local fishing-tackle shop and showing you the vast range of tackle which human ingenuity has devised to catch and land fish; not just rods and reels, but literally thousands of cunningly-designed devices and implements for presenting bait to fish and catching them; whether the fish are bottom-feeders or surface-feeders, and whether they live in freshwater or seawater.

I could be certain you would find that trip to the tackle shop interesting; not because I would have any expectation of interesting you in angling, but because I know that like any other human being, you are programmed by evolution with an inherent interest in tools, and the more ingenious those tools are, the better.

Manufacturers of consumer goods are well aware of this innate interest we all have in tools and processes. For one thing, they design objects which pander to our love of controlling processes and having ingenious tools at our command. Think of the way BMW puts some of its automobiles' controls *above* the front window, rather than around the steering wheel. Do they do this for logistical reasons? They would say yes, but isn't it much more likely they do it because we all know that airline pilots have controls above the front window as well as by the joystick, and BMW wants its customers to feel the sense of control and status that airline pilots presumably have?

They also build extensive – even excessive – functionality into their products. Think of the electronic devices you probably use: your mobile phone, your hi-fi system, your electronic calculator, your television remote control. Do you honestly use even half of the buttons these contain? Of course not. But would you have been so likely to buy the piece of equipment if it had considerably fewer features? Probably not.

It follows that an immensely powerful way to make your writing interesting is to give the reader *details*: details of processes, details of how things work, details of the features attached to a particular object. But it isn't enough to give all the dull, obvious details. Instead, you need to give the **dynamic details**.

By this I mean the exciting details; the ones that a reader will find interesting, the 'business end' of the process or object. If you're describing a tank, your reader is more likely to be interested in the speed with which it can cover rough terrain, and the power and range of its guns, than in the particular shade of paint used for the chassis.

71

If you're writing copy about a newly-built house for an estate agent's literature, your reader will find details about the number of rooms, the central heating and the features in the kitchen considerably more absorbing than a description of the type of bricks used in the foundations. There is no mystery about what the dynamic details are; it's really a matter of common sense.

Here are two examples of dynamic detail in action.

The first example is from one of the most popular thrillers published this century: the other is from the sales literature of one of the most resourceful and inventive clothing companies in the United States.

✍ EXAMPLE 20

Frederick Forsyth's masterly novel *The Day of the Jackal* is a great story, but its immense success is probably at least as much due to Forsyth's skilful use of dynamic detail as it is to his plot. In the novel, Forsyth pioneered the detailed explanation of numerous exciting processes which most thriller writers before him would have only summarised briefly. The result of his use of detail is that the reader is drawn into the world of the novel as a *participant* rather than – as is usually the case when reading fiction – as an *observer*.

By the end of the novel the reader knows, among other things, how to: obtain a forged British passport (note, however, that the method described in the book no longer works, as procedures have been tightened up); how to make contact with an illicit arms dealer; how to kill a man by breaking his neck; how to hide an assassin's rifle underneath a car; how to calibrate the sights of the rifle for maximum accuracy and how to operate using various illicit identities.

In this passage, the assassin, the Jackal, is meeting the man who has made him a special rifle he will use for the most important job of his career. The arms manufacturer is showing him some special explosive bullets, which have been designed to ensure that the Jackal can complete his mission with just one shot.

72

The Jackal knew about these bullets, although he had never had occasion to use them. Far too complex to be used en masse except if factory-produced, banned by the Geneva Convention, more vicious than the simple dum-dum, the explosive bullet would go off like a small grenade when it hit the human body. On firing, the droplet of mercury would be slammed back in its cavity by the forward rush of the bullet, as when a car passenger is pressed into his seat by a violent acceleration. As soon as the bullet struck flesh, gristle or bone, it would experience a sudden deceleration.

The effect on the mercury would be to hurl the droplet forwards towards the plugged front of the bullet. Here its onward rush would rip away the tip of the slug, splaying the lead outwards like the fingers of an open hand or the petals of a blossoming flower. In this shape the leaden projectile would tear through nerve and tissue, ripping, cutting, slicing, leaving fragments of itself over an area the size of a tea-saucer. Hitting the head, such a bullet would not emerge, but would demolish everything inside the cranium, forcing the bone-shell to fragment from the terrible pressure energy released inside.

Of course, much of the effect of this passage stems from the purpose of the explosive bullets: to obliterate a human being's head (by this point in the story we know that the human being is the former French president General de Gaulle). Still, I don't think anyone could deny that the fascination of this passage is substantially due to the detailed descriptions of explosive bullets and how they work.

Note, too, how Forsyth employs images which relate the unfamiliar world of ballistics to what is familiar to us. Phrases such as 'the fingers of an open hand', 'the petals of a blossoming flower', 'an area the size of a tea-saucer' almost literally bring the explosive bullets into our homes. That is what I mean by describing the reading experience as being that of a participant rather than an observer.

✍ EXAMPLE 21

The next example is from a mail order catalogue produced by the leading US clothing company, Patagonia. The piece, used to describe some of its travel clothes, was written by Nora Gallagher and Yvon Chouinard.

Here, the writers take something – travel clothing – which, unlike explosive bullets, is hardly inherently interesting, and *make* it interesting by giving the reader specific dynamic details which, in effect, take the clothing off the page of the catalogue and up a mountain, onto a kayak, or into a Bombay taxi. The passage is a fine example not only of the selection of dynamic detail but also of showing rather then telling.

You should also note the immense understanding the writers show of their readers' mentality, needs and dreams. Again: the more you know of what makes your readers tick, the more likely it is you will be able to write marketing copy that stuns them.

Travel clothes have always been a disaster. Made of shiny synthetics and weird knits, they have always bestowed on travellers the awful nom 'tourist'. To avoid even the suggestion of such a reputation, people will go to great lengths; the result is that they look like something the cat dragged in when they arrive in foreign hotels. Wrinkled Oxford shirts; heavy, hot blue jeans; blazers sodden and undone. If they look bad, they feel worse. And if their destination is any country south of San Francisco or west of Hawaii, they will be sure to be sweltering and disheveled by the second cup of morning tea.

We offer shirts for both men and women, trousers and a split skirt for women who must manoeuvre both foreign customs and foreign terrain. The money belts we make are classic, leather belts that will safely stash your cash whenever you travel among pickpockets, inflationary conditions, and American Expressless hotels. Last, but certainly not least, we designed a sports coat that can travel anywhere without ruining your good name. We call it our Travel Tweed.

Imagine if you were sailing around the world or climbing Mount Everest, you would need a sports coat for the Royal New Zealand Yacht Club or the embassy party after the climb. It shouldn't have mildewed or got moth-eaten in the hold, and it should come out of the pack relatively wrinkle-free.

This excellent, classic jacket is the cornerstone of Patagonia's Travel Line: practical clothing that goes from portages to palaces with equal aplomb. Other people have made wrinkle-free sports coats, but they always turned out so ugly as to be unwearable. We have searched the world for the perfect material and finally settled on a Japanese-made polyester tweed. It looks nothing like a polyester, has a soft hand* and comes in a brown tweed colour that goes well with dress khakis or Levis.

The Travel Tweed has a skeleton lining of tough, ripstop lining which won't grow ragged with wear or easily tear on a kayak or Bombay taxi. Its inside pockets are oversized to accommodate passports and maps; there is an outside chest pocket. Two flap-covered pockets at the lower front provide ample space into which one may shove one's fists when posing over newly ratified treaties or freshly made gins and tonics.

Instructions for folding the coat (essential for it to reach its full potential) are woven and sewn into the inside breast pocket so you won't lose them in the flight. The coat comes with its own ripstop travel pouch (11" x 11" x 1") to protect it from becoming soiled in your pack. We don't guarantee this coat to be 100 percent wrinkle-free, but at worst you may have to hang it up in in the bathroom while you shower so the wrinkles hang out.

That's a long piece, but in its own way as gripping as the extract from *The Day of the Jackal*. Now that you've read it, I think it's a fair bet you'll never look at travel clothing in quite the same way again.

---

* An American term meaning how a fabric feels to the touch.

3. Become moderately obsessive about choosing the best word

Expert writers are never satisfied until they have chosen exactly the right word to express what they want to say. The French novelist Gustave Flaubert used to call this word *le mot juste* ('the precise word') and reportedly spent hours trying to think of the right one.

But if finding the precise word is difficult in French, it is even more difficult in English, which – at least partly in consequence of its origins as a hybrid language combining Anglo-Saxon and Norman French – has a staggering array of synonyms and near-synonyms, plus a huge range of words which have both a concrete and figurative meaning.

The Polish-born novelist Joseph Conrad – who wrote in English even though it was only his *third* language after Polish and French – once said he preferred English to French because of the range of figurative meanings it offers. He gave as an example the word 'wooden', which in French simply means 'made of wood' but in English has a variety of connotations relating to something leaden and deadening.

As a writer of marketing copy, you most likely can't afford to spend hours searching for the precise word – or at least you probably can't unless you work in the creative department of an advertising agency. All the same, you *must* cultivate the discipline of taking real trouble over selecting the precise word for your own work. And if this means becoming moderately obsessive about the selection process, so be it.

Better to become moderately obsessive about your work and make your work astounding, than to be calm and indifferent to it and produce words that leave the reader equally calm and indifferent.

Fortunately you are not entirely alone in your quest to find the precise word. A thesaurus – which is not a species of dinosaur but a reference book listing synonyms and near-synonyms – can be immensely helpful when you know more or less what word you want, but need to know what other words are available (or wish to find a different word in order to avoid repetition).

Thesauruses are not a panacea; you may still not find the precise word you want in them; but they are immensely useful, and no serious writer should be without them. I strongly recommend you obtain a thesaurus which lists words alphabetically rather than according to word-classes (as the original *Roget's Thesaurus* does) because it will speed your rate of locating the word you want. To give you an idea of how useful and thorough a thesaurus can be; my Wordsworth Thesaurus, published by Wordsworth Editions Limited, has no less than forty-two synonyms or near-synonyms for the word 'precise'.

✎ EXAMPLE 22

Any of your favourite authors will provide you with numerous examples of use of the precise word. My own favourite example of exactness of expression is found in a short essay written by George Orwell: the author of, among other works, *Nineteen Eighty-Four* and *Animal Farm*. Orwell is a master of exact and economical expression, and if you haven't already read him, you've a treat in store.

One of his early journalistic pieces, *Bookshop Memories*, recounts his experiences of working in a bookshop when a struggling young writer. It's a splendidly entertaining essay throughout, and one passage contains an example of precise use of language which indicates Orwell's genius as clearly as *Eine kleine Nachtmusik*, *The Marriage of Figaro* or *The Magic Flute*, among others, makes us realise that Mozart was truly a gift of God.

Writing about the unpleasant aspects of bookshops, Orwell observes:

> As a rule a bookshop is horribly cold in winter, because if it is too warm the windows get misted over, and a bookseller lives on his windows. And books give off more and nastier dust than any other class of objects yet invented, and the top of a book is the place where every bluebottle prefers to die.

Can you spot the most brilliant word in this passage?

It is, of course, 'prefers'. Orwell could have written 'chooses', 'decides' or 'wants', but none of these would have had the wonderful force of 'prefers', which – beyond merely giving the blue-bottle a mind of its own ('chooses', 'decides' and 'wants' would also do that) – conveys the idea of the bluebottle carrying out a definite, concrete, decision to die on top of a book. It is a marvel-lously comic idea, and a perfect example of how, by not being sat-isfied by the first word that popped into his head (as I am sure the less remarkable words must have occurred to Orwell before he found the one that was just right), he produced something that was stunning rather than merely good.

4. Try to avoid repetition if you can

Apart from the short, common words (such as *and*, *or*, *if*, *but*, *the*, *a* and so on), repetition of a word too close to where it has already been used looks clumsy. Unfortunately, it isn't easy to specify exactly how close to a previous use of a word you can repeat the word and avoid your work having this clumsy feel to it. A good rule of thumb is that you ought to try to avoid repetition of the same word within about one page of A4 text, which in practice means about every 250–300 words, depending on whether you are typing or printing out in double-space or one and a half-space. Incidentally, I use one and a half-space myself, as it leaves plenty of room between lines for writing in corrections and improvements, and doesn't use as much paper as double-spaced writing does.

Every writer should be aware of their weak points; otherwise it's impossible to get better. Repetition is one of my particular stylis-tic weaknesses, and I pay a great deal of attention to eradicating it in revision.

Indeed, I tend to think repetition *should* be eliminated at the revision stage, rather than the writer getting tense about it and inhibiting the flow of words onto the page. Of course, with prac-tice you get into the habit of spotting repetitions and doing away with them even before they arise.

The best way of dispensing with repetitions is to use synonyms, which you can obtain from a thesaurus, or simply from your own knowledge of vocabulary.

Do be careful, though, to make sure that the words *are* syn-onyms and not near-synonyms; otherwise your meaning will be compromised. Bad as repetition is, you must never sacrifice meaning in order to avoid it.

As an example of how to avoid repetition, in the above few paragraphs I have used 'eradicate', 'eliminate', 'do away with' and 'dispense with' to describe the process of preventing repetition. My thesaurus gives the following synonyms for 'eliminate' in addition to the three I chose: *annihilate, bump off, cut out, delete, dispose of, disregard, drop, eject, exclude, expel, expunge, exterminate, get rid of, ignore, kill, knock out, liquidate, murder, omit, reject, remove, rub out, slay, stamp out, take out, terminate, waste.*

This list shows that, useful as a thesaurus can be, it isn't a substitute for thinking. Not all of these words or phrases would have been suitable in the context I required.

Remember, too, that bad as repetitions can be, they are often better than strangled attempts to avoid them. Your aim should be to write so that your reader is unaware you have made an effort to avoid a repetition.

Finally, bear in mind that deliberate repetition can often be highly effective as a way of hammering home a point. Winston Churchill's famous 'We shall fight on the beaches' speech owes much of its effect to the repetition of 'we shall fight'. Yes, here there is repetition, but it is **effective repetition**, because it adds to, rather than detracts from, the energy of the writing.

So how do you decide whether repetition looks clumsy or dramatic? This is one of those areas where you must rely on your own skill for assessing your work objectively and self-critically. The only help I can give you is to say that where the sense of what you are writing deliberately draws attention to your repetition, there is a good chance it will be effective, but that where the sense of what you are writing does not draw attention to your repetition, it is likely it will seem clumsy.

The problem of repetition doesn't arise with short, everyday words to anything like the extent it does with longer words. I'm not sure why this is so: I rather think the reader's brain is so used to these short, familiar words it doesn't absorb them with the same intensity it applies to longer words.

I don't mean that you can always repeat the shorter words with complete impunity; I just mean that as long as you aren't using the same short word about half a dozen times in one shortish paragraph, you'll probably be all right.

Incidentally, the same 'repetition immunity' which short, everyday words enjoy also tends to extend to the word 'said': a word you will often be using in your marketing copy where you want to quote a member of your organisation, or a third-party (such as a client). The brain tends to skip over 'said', so you can use it fairly often without worrying about it.

Certainly, repeating 'said' is far better than trying out the synonyms, most of which have a contrived feel to them. You don't need to bother with words like 'aver', 'affirm', 'state' and 'utter'. (I must confess that in a novel I wrote when at university, I used an even worse synonym for said: 'ejaculated'). Instead, stick to 'said'; varying it if need be with 'added' and, on occasion, 'commented'.

79

5. Avoid clichés

Your work must avoid clichés: those hackneyed expressions – most of them are metaphors or similes – which may have once meant something, but which have become so well-worn any life they once had in them has long been extinguished.

Here is an example of cliché in action:

✍ **EXAMPLE 23**

> *Even when it's raining cats and dogs, and cold as ice, and the people who wend their way past you look like death warmed up, you'll be as warm as toast and snug as a bug in a rug inside your Jarvis All-Weather waterproof raincoat.*

If you don't already own a Jarvis All-Weather waterproof raincoat, would this marketing copy be likely to make you buy one? I doubt it. 'Raining cats and dogs', 'cold as ice', 'wend their way', 'death warmed up', 'warm as toast' and 'snug as a bug in a rug' are all examples of clichés, and are pitifully weak as tools of expression.

The best way to avoid writing a cliché is to compose your own metaphor or simile. That way, you can be sure it won't have been used before, and even if what you write isn't so brilliant that it's taken up by the rest of humanity – and, fifty years or so later, becomes a cliché in its own right – at least you will show your reader you've taken the trouble to do your own thinking.

Rewriting the above example, you might end up with something like:

> *Even when it's raining like a Malaysian monsoon, and colder than the summit of Everest in winter, and the people who pass by you look as though they forgot to buy a lottery ticket on the weekend their numbers finally came up, you'll be as warm as a hot cross bun and snug as a comfortable cat inside your Jarvis All-Weather waterproof raincoat.*

These new metaphors and similes may not be stunning but they're all your own: no one can accuse you of not taking the trouble to devise some expressions that keep the reader interested.

80

By the way, when you do invent your own metaphors and similes, don't forget my earlier guidance that *brevity is the soul of wit*. In other words, don't create expressions which, while original, are obviously contrived. Such expressions draw attention to the ingenuity of the writer rather than amplify or energise the thing being described. These type of contrived expressions are horribly common in many first novels: the novelist's determination to be thought clever tends to take over from the need to make the writing come alive. What you get is something like:

> *Michael finally reached Susan's house at the top of Haverstock Hill. With no money at all, he had had no choice but to walk all the way from Greenwich. His feet ached like those of a polar bear which has trekked from Greenland to the North Pole, and then all the way back, after it discovers that the seals it was expecting to find at 90 degrees had not migrated north, after all.*

The comparison of Michael's feet to those of the polar bear is pretty shaky to start with, and by the end of the paragraph the image has become so contrived that we've forgotten about Michael and are in the far northern wastes, much too far from Susan and Haverstock Hill.

Remember that the point of using a metaphor or simile is to

grab, retain and focus your reader's attention, not to dissipate that attention on irrelevancies.

Which is a convenient lead-in to my final piece of general stylistic advice:

6. Stick to the subject

Even if you write with energy, conciseness, originality of expression and a careful attention to the precise meaning of what you say, your writing will still be weak and amateurish if you don't stick to your subject.

We have already seen that the stranger for whom you are writing will have no interest in you personally. If you don't astound him, fascinate him, he's going to switch you off.

Think of your reader as a passenger in the first class cabin of a transatlantic flight. There he sits, like a king, on his extra-wide seat with its extra leg room and ample arm rests. In front of him is the video monitor which is about to show the latest Arnold Schwarzenegger, Sylvester Stallone or Bruce Willis blockbuster; in his briefcase under his seat are three fat volumes which represent, respectively, two years' work by Messrs Crichton, Follett and Forsyth.

The hostess or steward hovers nearby, ready to offer him the eggs of the great Beluga sturgeon of the Volga and fine vintage champagne. He has your marketing literature on his lap. He is prepared to take a glance at it before indulging himself in pleasure.

How long do you think your window of opportunity – that brief interval during which you have his attention – will be open if you wander off your subject? Ten seconds? Fifteen? When you're competing with a movie that cost $100 million to make, a thriller that took two years to write, and with caviar and champagne? Well?

So *stick to your subject*. Don't digress, don't tease out points that don't need teasing out, don't wander off the path of maximum fascination. Keep giving your readers exciting images, punchy prose, original expressions: keep giving them a reason to stay on that path. You may not be as rich and famous as Messrs

Schwarzenegger, Stallone, Willis, Crichton, Follett and Forsyth, but writing is delightfully democratic: stick to your subject, give your reader your very best work, and you'll be read, and people will listen to what you say.

And quite soon you might be sitting on that extra-wide seat in first class *yourself*.

Textual guidance
■ ■ ■

We now move on to stylistic points which relate more to specific textual points than general advice.

I can't pretend to be able to give you a comprehensive list of every textual stylistic point that is likely to present a particular challenge. As we have seen, style is expression, and expression is ultimately a personal matter, as well as being as infinite as the universe.

Instead of purporting to be comprehensive, I have simply done what seems to me the only thing I can hope to do: compiled a list of the textual stylistic points I regard as representing particular challenges to *me*, and hope you will find my remarks useful for your own writing, too.

So here they are, in alphabetical order:

Adjectives

The secret of good use of adjectives is to use them sparingly.

The problem with adjectives is that they so easily become words that *tell*, rather than *show*. To that extent they are a kind of crutch. On the face of it they do your work for you and save you the job of bringing your writing alive. But only on the face of it; in reality they don't. It's like trying to create the character of the Toad by calling him irresponsible instead of bringing him to life by making him behave in an irresponsible fashion. It's like a holiday company describing its holidays as enjoyable in its brochure instead of giving its readers a vivid idea of the *experience* of going on one of its holidays.

You've probably been to one of those modern pub-restaurants – usually part of a nationwide chain – where most of the fittings are made of plastic and resin rather than wood, where the smiles on the faces of the waiters and waitresses are so bright you need sunglasses, and where the menus have all too obviously been written and designed by some trendy West End ad agency. Orange juice isn't orange juice, it's 'thirst-quenching' orange juice. Steaks aren't steaks, they're 'tender, mouth-watering' steaks. Eggs aren't eggs, they're 'farmfresh' eggs (just like the manure).

The menu is littered with so many adjectives that, when the meal finally arrives, good as it may be (I'm forced to admit that the food at most of these places isn't bad), it seems to bear about as much relation to what was described in the menu, as hamburgers on the posters in fast-food restaurants bear to the squashed object you get passed over the counter. The menu's adjectives have strangled the credibility and honesty of the place, like fast-growing weeds.

Yet this is only what is to be expected. Using words carries with it responsibility, and if you are irresponsible in the way you use words, you shouldn't be surprised if the result is that the time you have spent doing your writing has been wasted. In many cases – indeed, I'd go so far as to say in the great majority of cases – adjectives simply aren't necessary.

Shakespeare didn't write 'Shall I compare thee to a beautiful summer's day?', he wrote, 'Shall I compare thee to a summer's day?' He didn't have Macbeth say, 'Is this a sharp, deadly dagger which I see before me?' but 'Is this a dagger which I see before me?' True: the longer versions wouldn't have scanned, but we can be confident this wasn't the reason Shakespeare rejected the adjectives.

The Bard would have known instinctively that sharp, clear nouns or noun-phrases – such as a summer's day and a dagger – not only don't need a qualifying adjective before them, but would actually have their meaning diluted if one was used.

Please don't imagine I'm suggesting you don't use adjectives *at all* in your work: like any of the principles I suggest in this book, the guidance on adjectives is only that, guidance, and you must have sufficient responsibility as a writer to have the courage to break any rule that doesn't seem right to *you*. That would be true even if Shakespeare himself were writing this book: even he didn't know all the answers; he just knew more than anybody else has ever known, then or since.

It would sometimes be artificial to avoid an adjective. Also, you often need to use another noun to obtain the meaning you want, with the secondary noun playing a kind of adjectival role (such as *summer's* does in 'a summer's day'). All I am suggesting is that before you decide to use an adjective, test the sound of what you are writing to make sure that it doesn't sound better without it.

Adverbs

If adjectives are the crutches of writing, adverbs are the wheelchairs.

84

The only good thing to say about adverbs is that there is less temptation to use them when writing marketing copy than there is to use adjectives. When writing marketing copy you are more likely to want to describe an object or a person than how something is done.

On those occasions when you do feel an adverb coming on, treat it like a belch and try to suppress it if you can. In almost every case where you are tempted to use an adverb, you could, if you tried, do the job much better by expressing what you want to say in a different way.

Why should adverbs be such weak, lacklustre words? Ultimately I think the reason is that, like indiscriminately used adjectives, they don't give the reader any images, or any sense data, but just words that *assert* without offering the reader any reason to believe – or be convinced by – the assertion.

✍ EXAMPLE 24

For example, instead of saying:

The Stellar takes you to where you want to go quickly and comfortably

you should dump the adverbs and amplify the description to give the reader some hard evidence for believing what you want to say. The resulting rewrite could be read something like:

If it's speed you want, the Stellar's twin microjet turbine engines with afterburn will take you where you want to go at 150 mph as you recline in seats upholstered in finest wash leather.

Conjunctions

Conjunctions – by which I mean 'joining' words such as 'and', 'because', 'although', 'while' and so on – cause problems even to experienced writers.

Like adjectives and adverbs, they tend to be over-used. With the exception of 'and' – which is often, but by no means always, unavoidable – they are ugly words which contain an inherent, poisonous tendency to tempt you to make your sentences too long and sprawling.

My advice about conjunctions is that you should avoid them if you can. The best way to do so is to make two sentences when you were planning to make one. Alternatively, the conjunction can often be replaced by a semi-colon.

For example, instead of writing:

Anglers prefer Gibson's fishing-tackle because they know it'll help them increase the percentage of hooked fish which reach their landing-nets

you should write, simply:

Anglers prefer Gibson's fishing-tackle. They know it'll help them increase the percentage of hooked fish which reach their landing-nets

or else

Anglers prefer Gibson's fishing-tackle; they know it'll help them increase the percentage of hooked fish which reach their landing-nets

These last two versions have a crisp, clear ring to them which the sentence that incorporates 'because' doesn't have.

I must admit I regard 'because' and 'meal' as my two least favourite words in the language: they have a dull, dismal sound to them which I find most demoralising. And no, I'm not an anorexic; I like food. I'm talking about the word.

An almost equally ugly conjunction is 'although'.

> *Sales of our fishing-tackle have increased by more than 30 per-cent compared with the equivalent period last year, although two major new tackle suppliers entered the market in 1995.*

A long, dull sentence. Using 'even though' is better than 'although' in this example (as it often is) but it is even better if you start the sentence with the preposition 'despite' and write:

> *Despite two new tackle suppliers having entered the market in 1995, sales of our fishing-tackle have increased by more than 30 percent compared with the equivalent period last year.*

86

Note, incidentally, that I *didn't* write 'despite the fact that two new tackle suppliers have entered the market in 1995 ...' You'll see why a little later.

What about 'and'? Surely I'm not saying this should be avoided, too?

The answer is *yes*, if it joins two clauses which would be perfectly workable sentences in their own right, but *no* if it connects two nouns or adjectives.

So feel free to write, for example:

- Jack and Jill
- bucket and spade
- law and order
- crime and punishment
- love and marriage

but instead of writing, for example:

> *The new Novon has more than eight different attachments and is fully guaranteed for five years*

there is more force in breaking this one sentence up into two:

> *The new Novon has more than eight different attachments. It is fully guaranteed for five years.*

I think the reason why two simple sentences tend to have more impact than a complex one connected by 'and' is that the reader's brain likes to absorb the first point and then move onto the second. This is particular true where the 'and' connects two clauses with action in them.

> *This photograph shows supermodel Sandy Wood enjoying wearing our latest imitation mink jacket and the beaming smile on her face shows she is warm and snug in the coat, despite a temperature of minus twenty Centigrade.*

is much less effective than writing, simply:

> *This photograph shows supermodel Sandy Wood enjoying wearing our latest imitation mink jacket. The beaming smile on her face shows she is warm and snug in the coat, despite a temperature of minus twenty Centigrade.*

Like all the guidance I provide in this book, my suggestion that you should avoid 'and' to join two sentence-like clauses is not infallible. There may be cases where to use 'and' sounds better. Ernest Hemingway was famous for using 'and' to join clauses and thereby create a sense of fast-moving narrative. However, even he got it wrong sometimes, especially in his later work, where his frequent use of 'and' sometimes induces reader fatigue rather than excitement.

87

Should you start a sentence with a conjunction? My advice is that this is an area where you should follow the advice your teachers gave you, and avoid it. The only exception is that on occasion, where you want to create an effect of a sentence being dynamically linked to the preceding sentence, starting a sentence with 'and' can work. However, bear in mind that many of your readers will regard the use of 'and' at the start of a sentence as plain bad, however hard you try to make it appear dynamic.

'If'/'whether'

I have already pointed out that the written language tends to be more conservative than the spoken one. A consequence of this is that what is acceptable in speech is not always acceptable in writing.

An important example is the difference between 'if' and

'whether'. Many of us will say, for example:

I don't know if she's coming

The chairman asked if sales had increased since the decision to incorporate a built-in fragrance dispenser into the Novon.

Both these examples are fine if you are speaking, but in writing them you should replace 'if' with 'whether'.

But isn't this a contradiction to my basic premise that the written language is at its most effective when it resembles the spoken language, written down? Yes, but only a minor one. A certain amount of accommodation to the relative formality of the written language over the spoken is inevitable even for the most idiomatically-minded writer.

'Former'/'latter'

I hate these words, and so should you. They are clumsy, ugly and the biggest turn-off since the creation of the onion.

Avoid them at all costs. If you are thinking of saying, for example:

The managing director and the marketing director are both addressing the conference. The latter will be speaking before the former.

come to your senses and write anything, please, that doesn't involve the two dreaded words. In this example you could say:

The managing director and the marketing director are both addressing the conference, with the marketing director scheduled to speak before the managing director.

Here, the repetition of the job titles is a small price to pay for the avoidance of the two dreaded words.

Paragraphs

Good paragraphing is an essential part of good style. It is not an easy thing to get right, but you should find that after practice you are able to paragraph your work with sufficient expertise to be certain where the paragraph breaks ought to come.

The overriding rule for paragraphing is that you should start a new paragraph **wherever there is a distinct – even if only slight – change in the sense and/or the flow of what you want to say**.

This is the fundamental rule. It means you need to detect where the change in the sense or flow has come, and where you need to introduce a new paragraph. It is important to do your best to put the paragraph break in the most appropriate place; good paragraphing will help the reader onwards with the crucial process of obtaining meaning from what you write.

The difficulty with paragraphing is that often it will be a matter of opinion where the change in the sense/flow has taken place. Furthermore, different types of marketing copy will demand different approaches to paragraphing. For example, a punchy piece of advertising copy may be at its most effective if every sentence – or most of them – starts with a new paragraph. On the other hand, when you are writing a more sober, discursive article, you will want to paragraph in a correspondingly more restrained fashion.

My suggestion is that until you really get the hang of paragraphing you should be on guard to avoid making your paragraphs *too short*, rather than *too long*. Generally, a sequence of over-short paragraphs looks frivolous and silly, and quickly becomes irritating for the reader. Short paragraphs are all very well if you writing the kind of emphemeral, usually superficial stuff that tabloid newspapers contain, but you are writing copy which isn't designed to be left on the bus or on the train or thrown away; you are writing material which you hope will grab your reader's attention and keep grabbing it. To do this you need to put some depth, intelligence and drama in your work, and – other things being equal – you will make your job more difficult if your paragraphs are too short. You don't want your writing to have the surface froth but tastelessness of sparkling water; you want your work to be like quality vintage port: something that, once tasted, won't easily be forgotten.

However, you should certainly aim to *start* your work with a punchy, short first paragraph which grabs the reader's attention. As we see in the next chapter, this is particularly important for publicity material such as press releases and full-length articles, but the truth of it is that it is important for all kinds of writing.

Often the first paragraph of your work should be one-sentence long for maximum effect, but don't be slavishly bound by this dictum. Consider, for example, the first paragraph of Frederick Forsyth's *The Day of the Jackal*:

> It is cold at six-forty in the morning of a March day in Paris, and seems even colder when a man is about to be executed by firing squad. At that hour on 11th March 1963, in the main courtyard of the Fort d'Ivry, a French Air Force colonel stood before a stake driven into the chilly gravel as his hands were bound behind the post, and stared with slowly diminishing disbelief at the squad of soldiers facing him twenty metres away.

Who could read this without wishing to read on?

Forsyth could have made the first sentence into a paragraph of its own. This would have given the sentence an even greater impact, but would have lost the quick segue into the drama of the actual execution scene. On balance I think Forsyth was right to make the paragraph consist of two sentences rather than one.

If your marketing copy is to have maximum impact, you need to pay as much attention to your paragraphing as your favourite thriller-writers or novelists pay to theirs.

My recommendation that your paragraphs mustn't be too short doesn't mean you can inflict great wodges of text on your reader with impunity: you can't. Just as a succession of over-short paragraphs will irritate your readers, great unbroken paragraphs will also put them off, at least unless you have an extremely good reason for using them.

I think that is all the general guidance I should give you about paragraphing. It would be irresponsible of me to suggest a specific length your paragraphs ought to be: that is a highly individual and personal matter.

✍ EXAMPLE 25

Here are the opening six paragraphs of an article I wrote under a client's by-line. For convenience of analysis I have numbered them:

(1) The test of a truly revolutionary technology is that once we have it we are entirely dissatisfied with what we had before, and are unable easily to remember what our lives were like without it.

(2) Until the late 1960s millions of people watched black and white television without complaint, but replace someone's colour television now with a monochrome set and listen for the howls of protest.

(3) Technological innovation – particularly in the development of new devices to use in the home – has arguably been the greatest force for social change this century. Many problems have simply vanished under the onslaught of technological progress. The servant problem, which filled the correspondence columns of Victorian journals for decade after decade, has yielded to the vacuum cleaner, washing-machine, gas fire and effective household chemicals. The problem of what to do in the evenings after work has substantially been con-quered by television and other electronic entertainment. Television has its downside, of course, but it has probably done more to over-come what many regard as the inherent boredom of life than any development since the invention of the book.

(4) With technology offering such immense benefits, why are we so bad at making accurate assessments of the worth, or otherwise, of a technological innovation?

(5) I think the reason is that instead of investigating the innovation in a calm and objective frame of mind, we too often allow ourselves to be swayed by forces which, on the face of it, are mutually exclusive but are in fact related.

(6) These forces are a fundamental fear of technological innovation, and a reckless enthusiasm for it. They are related because when we fear something we suspend our rational judgement about it, and when we do that we are as likely to indulge in irrational enthusiasm as revul-sion. Religious cults work by making the cult member even more terri-fied of losing access to the 'benefits' of cult membership than he is of the inevitably all-too-human leader of the cult.

The reasons why I chose to paragraph the above copy in this way are as follows:

Paragraph 1: The article is about the need to recognise effec-tive technological innovation and encourage these innovations at an early stage. This first sentence emphasises the impact which successful innovation has on our lives. It is a fairly long sentence; I felt it would have maximum impact if it were a paragraph all on its own.

Paragraph 2: This sentence is deliberately designed to *illustrate* (i.e. show, rather than tell) the relatively abstruse point made in the first paragraph. I felt this sentence needed to be emphasised by having its own paragraph, too.

Paragraph 3: Here we plunge into the main argument of the article. I felt the readers needed some real meat to get their teeth into, and so made this paragraph fairly long. I could have started a new paragraph with the sentence beginning 'The servant problem,...' but I wanted to create a sense of *continuity of meaning*, so kept this, and the next two sentences, in the same paragraph.

Paragraph 4: When you use a question in this manner, as a way of ramming home the meaning of the article by making a direct appeal, it obviously makes sense to put the question into a paragraph of its own.

Paragraphs 5/6: I chose to spread this new phase of argument over two paragraphs in order to emphasise the fairly bold assertion in paragraph 5. However, this was mainly a matter of taste; it would have been reasonable to run these two paragraphs into one.

Note, generally, how my reasons for the way I chose to allocate this opening phase of the article into paragraphs are a combination of logic and taste. You may not agree with all my paragraphing decisions – and I am aware they are only one way of solving the problem – but they represented the best I could do by way of driving home my argument.

The final point to make about paragraphs relates to the paragraphing of direct quotations, which you will need to introduce into your marketing copy when you wish to give the impression of setting down what someone actually says: something you will often want to do in publicity material (such as press releases and full-length articles) and in newsletters.

In most cases you ought to follow the style of fiction writers, who start a new paragraph when they set down dialogue. In this case, I tend to introduce the quotation after a colon.

Consider the following example, which could, possibly, come from a corporate newsletter:

Addressing the shareholders, Sir John Buck-Trumpington said:
  'Ever since my great-grandfather founded this company in 1875, we have been pursuing a policy of greed, unfair competition and harassment of our employees. My family and I are all multi-millionaires. I see no reason whatsoever to change an approach which has been so successful.'

Paragraphs containing direct quotations should not be too long, so if you are going to let this charming old fellow ramble on a little more, consider creating a new paragraph. You can introduce this with something like 'he added' or 'he also said'.

Note that if you *don't* introduce the follow-on paragraph with an introductory phrase, the correct punctuation method is not to close the inverted comma (or commas) in the preceding paragraph. Only close the inverted commas when the quotation is complete.

93

For example:

Addressing the shareholders, Sir John Buck-Trumpington said:
  'Ever since my great-grandfather founded this company in 1875, we have been pursuing a policy of greed, unfair competition and harassment of our employees. My family and I are all multi-millionaires. I see no reason whatsoever to change an approach which has been so successful.
  'In my view the trouble with the modern business world is that workers expect to be paid for doing a day's work.'
  Sir John added: 'I strongly recommend that a maximum wage of two pence an hour be introduced with immediate effect for all employees – including the directors – who are not members of the Buck-Trumpington family. By the way, does anybody in the hall have an impressive rhododendron hedgerow they need trimming? If so, I'd be happy to cut it for them '
  After Sir John was led off the stage by two young men in white coats who had brought him from the Twilight Days Nursing Home, Digby Buck-Trumpington, chairman of Trumpington Tiles plc, stood up and said:
  'I must, as I am obliged to do each year, apologise profusely for my

uncle's remarks. As many of you know, he retired some years ago and has not been well.'

He added: 'I should explain to those of you who have never been to our Annual General Meetings before, that under the terms of my great-great grandfather's will, the oldest living male member of the Buck-Trumpington family must be given the opportunity to address shareholders at the Annual General Meeting.'

Prepositions

Prepositions present two principal stylistic challenges:

1. Should you end a sentence with them?

At school you were probably taught you shouldn't do this. My advice is that your teachers were right. Ending a sentence with a preposition always looks ugly, and you can invariably find a better way of expressing what you want to say.

The problem of ending a sentence with a preposition arises because so many English verbs use one or two prepositions to give them new areas of meaning. However, it isn't good stylistically to write something like:

> *After the meeting, Peter Drake, whose investment company owns more than five percent of shares in Trumpington Tiles, said that the outrageous annual interjections by Sir John were something he was no longer prepared to put up with.*

Here, you can simply use 'tolerate' to replace 'put up with'. Often the recasting is less straightforward than this, but recasting is always possible.

2. The split infinitive

This, one of the oldest and most-disputed problems of English style, arises because, unlike – so far as I am aware – any other European language, apart from Romanian, English uses a preposition as part of the infinitive (e.g. 'to eat', 'to go', 'to write'). The result is that when you use an adverb with an infinitive, the 'to' often becomes separated from the rest of the infinitive. This is known as the split infinitive and is regarded as poor style.

The reason why there is so much debate about the split infinitive is that splitting the infinitive often actually sounds less clumsy than not splitting it. Certainly we usually split it in everyday speech. However, this is another example of where we must abide by the greater formality of the written language.

A famous example of the split infinitive is found at the start of the original series of the TV show *Star Trek*, where the voice-over describes the aim of the voyages of the Star Ship 'Enterprise' as being, among other things, *to boldly go where no man has gone before.*

'To boldly go' is a split infinitive. However, saying 'boldly to go' would have sounded pedantic and slightly absurd.

Fortunately, avoiding the split infinitive does not always sound as bad as 'boldly to go' sounds. My advice is to avoid the split infinitive in your writing if you can, but not to be afraid of using it if necessary.

95

As a brief interlude from instructional guidance: can you construct a meaningful sentence in English which ends with *seven* consecutive prepositions?

Try this one, which is the plaintive whine of a little boy whose mother proposes to read to him at bedtime from a book about Australia:

'Mum, what did you bring that book that I didn't want to be read out of about Down Under up for?'

'Start'/'begin'

Be careful with these words. Used as verbs, they are commonly thought of as being interchangeable. In fact their meanings differ slightly, but significantly.

'Start' has a somewhat more dynamic, active meaning than 'begin'.

For example, the advertising strapline *Start the day with Mellors' muesli* makes the muesli seem like a potent addition to your life-force. On the other hand, if you wrote *Begin the day with Mellors' muesli* it sounds as though you'll still be half-asleep even after eating a good bowlful.

Similarly, 'start' as a noun is stronger than 'beginning'.

There's no better start to the day than Mellors' muesli

is much stronger than

There's no better beginning to the day than Mellors' muesli

But use 'beginning' where you want to avoid any sense of dynamism or excitement:

From beginning to end, the Bossington village embroidery contest was characterised by a spirit of fair play.

The greater strength of 'start' over 'begin' or 'beginning' stems from its association with 'start' in the sense of 'make a sudden movement'.

'That'

96

Be careful not to over-use the word 'that'. When it is employed to introduce indirect speech or as a relative pronoun, *it can often be omitted*, with a resulting improvement to the flow and conciseness of your work.

For example:

    a *The managing director said that 1995 had been a record year.*

can be rewritten as

The managing director said 1995 had been a record year.

which is neater and better.

    b *There was no sign of the consignment that they had ordered.*

can be rewritten as

There was no sign of the consignment they had ordered.

I suggest, when you revise your work, you eliminate every 'that' which can be struck out without spoiling the sense of your work.

Incidentally, 'who/which/that is' and 'who/which/that are' can also often be eliminated with an improvement in conciseness.

The new recruits who are starting work next week must attend a seminar that is scheduled to start on Monday at 09.00 sharp.

can be rewritten as

The new recruits starting work next week must attend a seminar scheduled to start on Monday at 09.00 sharp.

'The best possible'

I have already advised you to do your utmost to avoid the dreaded expression 'the best possible', or indeed this expression with any superlative.

It's horribly common in business literature, and indicates that the writer has run out of ideas.

A typical example of the phrase in action would be:

We pride ourselves on giving you the best possible service.

which is about as genuine as the smile of a prostitute, the tears of a crocodile, and the friendship of a rattlesnake.

97

Basically, 'the [superlative] possible' is like those stupid phrases – such as 'how long is a piece of string?' and 'it's a question of horses for courses' – which businesspeople use when they don't want to bother using the set of neurones and synapses between their ears. If you are ever tempted to write 'the [superlative] possible', or indeed either of the other two phrases, spend a few seconds reflecting that it's taken your brain four billion years to evolve from primitive amino acids into the most remarkable object in the known universe, and for heaven's sake write something more interesting.

'The fact that'

'The fact that' is another phrase you should avoid at all costs. It's clumsy, slow and dull. Fortunately, you can always rewrite so as to eliminate it.

For example:

'The fact that we've always made a substantial profit from selling gerbils directly to schools doesn't mean we shouldn't explore the possibility of selling to pet shops,' said Mr Rufus Squeak, managing director of Gorgeous Gerbils Ltd.

Here, you can replace 'the fact that' with 'just because'. You should get into the habit of replacing 'the fact that' in the composition stage, even before you set it down on paper.

'Very'

Don't use it. In many cases it's a redundant intensive: you're better off just using the adjective; and in the remaining cases it tends to devalue the whole meaning of what you want to say. There's something silly and irritating about the word: like those cheap tricks you find in joke shops.

When you really do want to intensify an adjective, use 'extremely'.

Active versus passive construction

An active construction is one where the logical subject of the action is also the grammatical subject of the assertion. For example:

The research and development unit developed this new drug.

A passive construction is one where the emphasis is put not on the subject of the sentence but on the agent of the action (to achieve this the verb will have to be modified and usually the word 'by' will have to be used).

This new drug was developed by the research and development unit.

There are sometimes occasions where it is stylistically better to use a passive construction. Generally, this occurs where the agent is more surprising or interesting than the subject of the sentence. For example:

The new consignment of paperclips was stolen by a gang of ruthless robbers.

You will also need to use the passive form of the verb where you are unsure who was the agent of the action.

The paperclips were stolen.

However, in the vast majority of cases an active construction carries with it far more force than a passive construction. Use the active form unless you are absolutely convinced the passive form sounds better.

For example:

Alexander Graham Bell invented the telephone.

is much more effective as a sentence than

The telephone was invented by Alexander Graham Bell.

'We' as the corporate body

Finally, if you're writing a corporate brochure or newsletter, don't be tempted to use the first person plural. It's okay for an advertising strapline or for lightweight advertising copy, but it doesn't work when you're writing something more extensive and formal.

Use of the first person plural soon becomes clumsy and tired in a non-advertising context.

99

> *As one of the leading global custodians in the world, we at Boyle's Bank strive to maximise income from our clients' overseas investments. We use a wide range of standard and value-added custody services, which we deliver to our clients by the very latest electronic communication technology.*

In this kind of example it is always better to avoid the first person plural and instead to use the third person, which helps to give the writing a sense of authority and formality.

> *As one of the leading global custodians in the world, Boyle's Bank strives to maximise income from its clients' overseas investments. It uses a wide range of standard and value-added custody services, delivered to clients by the very latest electronic communications technology.*

The second version has a more authoritative and professional ring to it. The style is objective and dispassionate: exactly the style an objective journalist would use.

Note, incidentally, that a company, corporation or firm is always third person *singular*, not *plural*, even if it has a plural form.

For example, write

Boyle's Bank believes in quality service.

and not 'Boyle's Bank *believe* in quality service.'

and write

Raleigh Brothers encourages initiative on the part of staff.

and not 'Raleigh Brothers *encourage* initiative on the part of staff'.

KEY LEARNING POINTS

- Forget about deliberately cultivating a style; concentrate on communicating what you want to say as clearly as you can.

- *Show* your readers what you mean, don't *tell* them.

- Know your readers.

- Use imagery and detail to add excitement to your work.

- Find the word which expresses precisely what you need to say.

- Avoid repetition.

- Don't use clichés.

- Use adjectives sparingly.

- Avoid using adverbs.

- Use conjunctions as little as possible.

- Use active rather than passive constructions.

4

. . .

Writing publicity material

Introduction

■ ■ ■

In this chapter and the four that follow it, I look at specific kinds of marketing copy and suggest how you should set about writing each one. In other words, I will propose how the principles that have formed the substance of the book so far can be applied to the challenge of crafting a particular type of marketing copy.

My approach is to suggest the following to you for each type:

1. What the purpose of the copy should be.

2. The typical readership.

3. What you have to know about the product and/or organisation in order to write the copy.

4. What a typical blueprint of the copy should be.

With one exception, I conclude each analysis with a real-life or imaginary example. I use real-life examples wherever it seems instructive to do so, but imaginary examples where this seems a better procedure, or where using real examples might lead to copyright problems.

A word about the aim of providing you with a blueprint.

The overriding idea of this book is that writing is both an art and a science. It follows that while there is plenty of factual information that needs to be assimilated when learning to write well, ultimately no book which contains instructional guidance on writing can hope to provide you with all the knowledge and expertise you need in order to become a competent writer.

In the end, when you write you are on your own, with your only resources your vocabulary, your knowledge of grammar, your instinctive feel for what will sound good on the page, and your determination to produce your very best work. A book such as this cannot be a substitute for those crucial personal skills; it can, however, be an invisible friend who stands behind you when you write and looks over your shoulder, and who even goes so far as to suggest to you what words and phrases are likely to succeed or fail.

More than this, it can suggest to you what kind of basic structure a particular piece of marketing copy ought to have. This is precisely what I suggest when I provide the blueprints.

The blueprint is not supposed to be a dogmatic, inflexible guide. If your own experience and feel for what you are doing tells you that you wish to approach the challenge in another way, fair enough. Sooner or later you will want to discard the blueprints anyway, but I hope this will only be when you are sufficiently skilled as a writer of marketing copy to know exactly what effect you wish to achieve, and how to achieve it. In that case I will be happy, because this book will have achieved its purpose.

Writing marketing copy: the golden rule

Before you start writing any piece of marketing copy, imagine you are the reader. What would the reader want to *read*? What would the reader want to *know*?

Write for that reader.

Some don'ts

Don't insult your reader's intelligence by explaining things which don't need explaining.

Don't think the reader won't mind if you slip in crude, boastful, unsubstantiated references to your organisation's or client's expertise and the high quality of their products or services. You have to convey all this by showing, not just by baldly *telling*.

Don't write in a pompous, affected way. Be yourself. Be natural.

Don't forget what you've learned in the first three chapters of this book.

The press release
■ ■ ■

Purpose

The reason for writing a press release is to get as much coverage in the press as you possibly can of whatever you want to publicise.

To do this your press release has to be absorbing from start to finish. Remember that editors get dozens more press releases than they can actually use (sometimes *hundreds* more). Not only does this mean yours has to be superb if it is going to be used; it also means your cherished press release will probably be scrutinised for less than ten seconds before being set aside for publication or binning.

Even if your release *does* pass the initial selection stage, it is unlikely to be used in its entirety. In the vast majority of cases, the best you can expect is that the editor publishes the first three or four paragraphs, or edited versions of them.

Typical readership

The real readers of your press release are not the readers of the journals or newspapers – or even the audiences of the radio or television stations – to which you are directing the release, but the editors (or programme directors) of these media. This is because in most cases, even if your release is used it will be rewritten, edited or cut before being published.

Your typical readership will therefore depend on the media in which you want your news story to appear.

Remember that there are probably many more media in which your story *should* appear than you know about. Make sure you consult a media directory, which will provide comprehensive contact details, with the listings set down according to different categories. An excellent media list I can recommend is supplied by the London-based organisation PIMS. You can either buy a single copy of this or subscribe to it on a regular basis.

What you need to know about the product and/or organisation

You need to know what the news angle is and enough about the product and/or organisation to be able to write about it interestingly.

Blueprint

Above all, you must make sure you get the newsworthiness of your release right there upfront. The first paragraph *must* contain the news story in summary, with subsequent paragraphs elaborating on the story, but never wandering off the subject.

Keep your press releases short. They should never be more than a couple of pages of A4 in length.

Also, make sure you print or type the text in double spacing or one and a half spacing. That way, the editor or sub-editor can if necessary edit the release directly onto the paper on which it appears and then pass it for publication.

Give your release a sober, factual *headline* which summarises the entire story as succinctly as you can. *Don't* try to provide a clever, punning headline of the type you often see in newspapers or magazines: your own idea of what is witty or funny may not coincide with the editor's. Even if it does, editors, like Groucho Marx, prefer to keep the funny lines all to themselves.

You must also *date* your release. Some writers, including myself, like to put 'For Immediate Release' at the head of the release, but this is optional. If the news your release contains is highly time-critical (such as if it is price-sensitive information issued by a company listed on a stock exchange) you may want to indicate a time embargo at the top of the page; but if the information is not time-critical indicating an embargo would seem pretentious.

My recommendation is that you confine yourself to a maximum of six paragraphs for the actual release, with these paragraphs having the following functions:

1. A short, succinct, exciting statement of your news story. By the way, avoid starting a press release with 'The': try to think of a more dynamic start.

2. First elaboration of your news story, bringing in other key facts the reader is likely to want to know.

3. Second elaboration of your news story, bringing in additional material of interest.

4. Provision of background information to your story.

5. Quotation from someone involved in the story. If necessary you can invent the actual words, but check them with the person first.

6. Wrap-up and conclusion. A good way of doing this is to suggest unexplored possibilities for the future.

Write '-ends-' at the end of the main copy. That way, the editor knows there are not one or more other pages which have gone astray.

Finally, make sure you give a contact name and number whom the editor or journalist can ring to obtain further information.

✍ EXAMPLE 26

For Immediate Release   **March 7 1876**

MAJOR NEW COMMUNICATIONS DEVICE PATENTED

A new communications device which looks set to revolutionise the way people talk to one another has been patented today by a Boston-based Scottish-American speech expert, Alexander Graham Bell.

The device, known as the 'telephone' – from the Greek roots *tele*, 'far' and *phone*, 'sound' – uses electricity to enable people to speak to one another over distances beyond earshot. The invention creates the possibility that one day, if certain technical obstacles can be mastered, any human being may be able to speak to another human being, anywhere in the world.

Bell, whose family moved to the United States in 1870, is already well known as a teacher of the deaf, and an instructor of such teachers. A pioneer in the art of teaching the deaf to speech, Bell has for several years been working on devices which exploit the potential of electricity to carry sound impulses. He has long believed that a device to enable humans to talk to one another at a distance may be possible, but it is only during the past few years that he has succeeded in bringing his ideas to practical fruition.

The basic principle of the telephone is that a transmitter uses a diaphragm placed against a variable resistor to translate the fluctuations in air pressure produced by a speaker's voice into changes in the strength of an electric current. This varying electric current is relayed through wires to a receiver, where it is translated back into sound waves by the interaction of an electromagnet and another diaphragm, which vibrates in response to the fluctuations of current in the electromagnet.

As a modest man, Bell does not wish to be quoted, but his assistant Thomas Watson said, 'This invention is the greatest thing since we left the Ark. The day's coming, though maybe not in our own lifetimes, when men will be a universal brotherhood using the telephone to talk to one another around the globe.'

Considerable interest has already been expressed in the telephone by ordinary people and large commercial organisations. The possibility exists to create a telephone 'exchange', whereby calls will be capable of being routed between different people without the necessity of their having their own exclusive line. The principle of the telephone exchange appears to make Watson's predictions realistic.

-ends-

For further information please contact:

Thomas A. Watson
Bell Telephone Company

Tel: 1

107

The 'thoughtpiece' article

■ ■ ■

Purpose

The thoughtpiece article is an extremely powerful publicity device. Its purpose is to obtain a considerable amount of free coverage in a newspaper or journal read by your organisation's or client's existing and/or potential customers.

You normally can't achieve this by sending the newspaper or journal a lengthy account of your products and/or organisation, because the media in question isn't in the business of promoting your organisation and simply won't publish it. Of course, you could send them an advertisement, but placing an advertisement costs money.

An ingenious solution to this problem – which I have found to score a high success rate in terms of obtaining coverage – is to prepare an article about a subject which the newspaper's or journal's editor and readers are likely to find interesting – and which also fits in with the business activities of the organisation you are publicising – and submit this for publication.

You normally can't say anything too explicit about the organisation in this kind of article but you *can* expect the article to be attributed to a named person at your organisation or client, and for the organisation or client to be mentioned as well. The attribution will position the organisation as a leading one in the industry, and by extension as a firm with which the readers ought to be doing business.

Of course, it is perfectly acceptable for you to ghost-write the article and for it to appear under the by-line of someone else (ideally someone fairly senior) at the organisation.

It is usually fairly easy to place these articles, as long as they *are* sincere, objective thoughtpieces and not just thinly-disguised self-promotion. But do be careful to submit the article to only one competing journal at a time; there's no reason why you shouldn't send the article to more than one media, but they mustn't be journals which are competing for the same readership. Editors get extremely annoyed if they are publishing a piece which is appearing at about the same time in a competing publication, and they tend to have long memories.

Your aim in writing the thoughtpiece article must be to write to the standard, or beyond, of the media's own journalists.

Typical readership

This will depend entirely on the readership of the media in which you manage to place the article. Before you submit the article, you must be certain that the media in question is read by people you want to influence in your organisation's, or client's, favour.

What you need to know about the product and/or organisation

You need to know what kind of viewpoint or attitude the article should take in order to provide maximum benefit to your organisation or client.

Often it is possible to adopt an attitude or belief in the article which, while projected sincerely and convincingly in the article, has been deliberately chosen to be to the organisation's advantage.

For example, if your organisation or client were in the business of supplying open computer systems, your article could focus on the advantages and benefits, *generally*, of using these systems.

If you are ghost-writing the article, you will in most cases need to obtain ideas from the person to whom it will be attributed when it is published. Ideally it should be something of a collaboration between you and the person to whom it is attributed. After all, it is appearing under their name, and they will want to feel it is at least partly their own work.

Blueprint

It would be absurd for me to give you a paragraph-by-paragraph blueprint for a thoughtpiece article. These articles can take so many forms and be written in so many ways that any dogmatic blueprint would be far too restrictive.

I do, however, have two important suggestions.

1. Before you start writing the article, get clear in your mind exactly what you want to say. Once you've done this, telephone the editor of the newspaper or journal in question and whet his or her interest in the piece before you write it. You must also find out how many words the article ought to be in length. Stick closely to the specified wordage or range of wordage.

2. It is *essential* you follow a clear, logical line of reasoning throughout the article, and that no extraneous material or irrelevant digressions are included.

I tend to write my articles around the following blueprint:

Stage 1: Statement of the problem

Stage 2: Elaboration of the problem

Stage 3: Resolution of the problem.

I would tentatively suggest that Stage 1 should occupy about one-quarter of the length of your article, Stage 2 about one-half, and Stage 3 about one-quarter. These are only guidelines, and they are not cast in stone. In fact, in the example I provide below, the first and third stages are somewhat shorter than this, and the middle stage rather longer. You have to proceed by instinct, not by rule.

One piece of advice that *does* amount to a rule: **make sure your article has an arresting start**. You really need to make an effort to give your article a start that will interest your readers from the word go.

In my experience I have found there to be three principal ways of doing this. I am not suggesting these are the only ways; I am only saying these have worked for me. They are:

1. The exciting image

Use an image which is likely to catch your readers' attention. The image must, however, be *appropriate*; otherwise your readers will be conscious you chose it in order to catch their attention.

So, if you were writing an article which argued the case that more people ought to reduce the amount of cash they carry when shopping and carry an electronic funds transfer at point of sale (EFTPoS) card instead, you might start by saying:

> *Carrying too much cash is like doing your shopping in the nude. You have no protection, and ultimately you look pretty silly.*

Examples 18 and 19 above are also illustrations of the use of the exciting image to start an article: both these cases are articles I published under my own name.

2. The bold assertion

Here, you start your article with a bold – but truthful and sensible – assertion. For example, if I were writing a thought-piece article to promote the idea that would-be writers ought to spend more time taking the trouble to read books about how to write, I might start by saying:

> *We no more instinctively know how to write than we know instinctively how to read. We have to learn both skills. As writing is so much more difficult than reading, why aren't people prepared to spend correspondingly more effort on mastering it than they are on mastering reading?*

Here, I have elaborated the first assertion into a second assertion which is a rhetorical question (a question you pose for dramatic effect, rather than because you want someone to tell you the answer). Rhetorical questions can be highly effective in thoughtpiece articles, but don't overdo them, or your reader really will begin to feel you need some answers. One or two such questions per article will suffice.

3. The external reference

Here, you bring in an interesting external reference right at the start in order to grab your readers' attention. The external reference will typically be to a person, book, film, sport or other popular reference with which you can be sure your readers will be familiar.

For example:

> 'We shall fight on the beaches' said Winston Churchill, but even he wouldn't have been keen to fight on some of Britain's beaches, which are so polluted even the lugworm have decided to beat a retreat.

111

This might be the start of an article which argued the need to bring in tougher regulations for beach cleanliness. The image of the lugworm is a secondary hook to grab the readers' attention: like the reference to Churchill, the image is slightly comic. Both ideas are of course exaggerations: we know Churchill wouldn't really have excluded dirty beaches from his call to arms, just as we know that some lugworms would remain on even the most polluted beaches. But the effect we want is gained, and the poetic licence is justifiable. After all, you're writing exciting marketing copy, not an encyclopaedia.

✍ EXAMPLE 27

To illustrate the principles of the thoughtpiece article, here is the full text of the article, the beginning of which I have already analysed in the previous chapter under the section on paragraphing.

I wrote the article on behalf of a client which is in the business of supplying high-quality banking technology to financial institutions.

I was keen to position the client as a leading authority on delivering practical technological innovation. I therefore wrote an article on this subject. The article contains no overt promotion of my client; the idea was to obtain the promotion subtly, through the attribution of the article to a named person at my client, with the client's name also being mentioned.

In the following example, for convenience, I have marked the three stages of the argument.

In this article the opening technique is the bold assertion.

HOW WE CAN MASTER THE ART OF ASSESSING A TECHNOLOGICAL INNOVATION

(Stage 1: Statement of the problem)

The test of a truly revolutionary technology is that once we have it we are entirely dissatisfied with what we had before, and are unable easily to remember what our lives were like without it.

Until the late 1960s millions of people watched black and white television without complaint, but replace someone's colour television now with a monochrome set and listen for the howls of protest.

Technological innovation – particularly in the development of new devices to use in the home – has arguably been the greatest force for social change this century. Many problems have simply vanished under the onslaught of technological progress. The servant problem, which filled the correspondence columns of Victorian journals for decade after decade, has yielded to the vacuum cleaner, washing-machine, gas fire and effective household chemicals. The problem of what to do in the evenings after work has substantially been con-quered by television and other electronic entertainment. Television has its downside, of course, but it has probably done more to over-come what many regard as the inherent boredom of life than any development since the invention of the book.

With technology offering such immense benefits, why are we so bad at making accurate assessments of the worth, or otherwise, of a tech-nological innovation?

I think the reason is that instead of investigating the innovation in a calm and objective frame of mind, we too often allow ourselves to be swayed by forces which on the face of it are mutually exclusive but are in fact related.

These forces are a fundamental fear of technological innovation, and a reckless enthusiasm for it. They are related because when we fear something we suspend our rational judgement about it, and when we do that we are as likely to indulge in irrational enthusiasm as revulsion. Religious cults work by making the cult member even more terrified of losing access to the 'benefits' of cult membership than he is of the inevitably all-too-human leader of the cult.

(Stage 2: Elaboration of the problem)

The trouble with the fear of technology is that it is intellectually respectable. George Orwell's *Nineteen Eighty-Four* is a typical example of a work which gains much of its effect by pandering to the fear people have of an oppressive technological future. While the book is surprisingly devoid of references to advanced technology – there is no mention of computers, for example, although these were fairly well known in 1948, when the novel was written – Orwell does give us the telescreen: a compulsory feature of every house (except for those belonging to the proles). The telescreen functions in sinister fashion both as a means of broadcasting pictures and sound and also as a way of relaying live images to the authorities of whoever is in the room.

113

Orwell was a dying and despairing man when he wrote *Nineteen Eighty-Four*, but it remains remarkable that someone as knowledgeable about practical matters as he could see no reason for optimism about Man's technological progress. The idea that the telescreen, or television, might be a source of pleasing entertainment to millions after a hard day's work appears beyond either his unconscious or conscious imagination.

Similarly, one of the many themes central to *Nineteen Eighty-Four* is the physical squalor of the characters' lives, yet it never appears to occur to Orwell that technology could make an immense contribution to improving life in so many aspects; to meeting, in effect, the consumer's most fundamental needs for convenience, comfort and security.

In adopting such a pessimistic view of technological progress, Orwell was merely following not only the major intellectual trend of his time, but also the view most people adopt towards innovation. Even now, most intellectuals are cynical (or at least pretend to be) about technological innovation. The vast majority of popular books and films produced this century, from *Brave New World* to *Terminator 2*, embody this cynicism. Even *2001: A Space Odyssey*, whose ostensible theme is the elevation of mankind by alien beings whose technology is infinitely more advanced than our own, features HAL, the computer who is also a mass murderer.

Yet an antipathy towards technological innovation is not the prerogative of writers and film-makers. Most people initially distrust innovation, even those who ought to know better.

In these days of mega-hype over the launch of Windows 95, it is pertinent, and amusing, to remember that the main reason Bill Gates got Microsoft underway was that in the late 1970s, IBM did not believe personal computer software to be of any commercial significance. In fact, IBM's comments on technological innovation have often turned out to be delightfully ironic. Less than twenty-five years ago, IBM predicted that the world market for computers was only about 100,000 machines.

Still, IBM's rivals have often not done much better. In the 1970s, a senior manager of DEC told the World Future Society at its convention in Boston that there was no reason why an individual would want a computer in his home. The probability now is that by the new century, more than a billion people around the world will have access to a personal computer, either at work or at home.

Charles Babbage (1791–1871) suffered greatly from a distrust among many of his most illustrious contemporaries of his ambitious plans to build what was essentially a digital computer constructed from gearwheels and levers. This distrust probably set the evolution of computers back by fifty years. In 1832, the Astronomer Royal, Sir George Bidell Airy, was asked to evaluate Babbage's work and decide whether the Government should continue funding it. Airy pronounced the work 'worthless'; funding was withdrawn and Babbage was forced to give up.

The idea that Babbage was scuppered by the lack of precision components is a misconception: the problem was not that Victorian engineering couldn't machine the parts to the requisite tolerances but rather that Babbage required large numbers of components and making these was extremely expensive in an age that had no mass-production of high-precision parts.

That Babbage's ideas would have worked was proved in 1991, when two engineers at London's Science Museum completed the construction of Difference Engine 2, a highly ambitious forerunner of Babbage's even more complex Analytical Engine. They used modern components produced by modern mass-production methods, but worked to Babbage's original plans and to his specifications for precision. Difference Engine 2 is in the permanent computing exhibition at the Science Museum. The machine works perfectly, which suggests that if the Astronomer Royal's decision had been different, Windows

95 might have been known as Windows 45.

Nor is the widespread failure of imagination which so often applies to technological innovation by any means confined to attitudes people hold towards computers. In 1879, Sir William Preece, then chief engineer of the Post Office, testified to a Select Committee of the House of Commons that the telephone – the technical feasibility of which was already established – had little future in Britain. 'In America the absence of servants has compelled Americans to adopt communications systems', he said. 'Here in Britain we already have a superabundance of messengers.' Not to be outdone, the US Postmaster General was subsequently to turn down an offer by Samuel Morse to sell the government the rights to his telegraph for $100,000.

Yet all these observations are, in effect, wisdom in hindsight. In our age of ever-escalating technological innovations, one of the most pressing challenges that faces us is how to cultivate an attitude towards technology which encourages successful innovation while weeding out ideas which are technological dead-ends, or – worse – which force a technology on consumers or on organisations when there is no real need for the application.

The banking technology industry is one where experience has shown that an application of technology will be successful if the application drives the technology, rather than vice versa. Automated teller machines (ATMs) and electronic funds transfer at point of sale (EFTPoS) didn't achieve a dramatic success because the communications and verification technology on which they depend suddenly became available. No, it was because the availability of this technology coincided with a new demand on the part of banks' customers for access to their funds around-the-clock and at many locations other than bank branches, as well as a demand for means of paying for goods without using cheques or cash.

The next major technological innovation on the horizon in the banking technology sector is the smart card, which offers the prospect of huge advantages in terms of greatly improved card security (unlike magnetic stripe cards, smart cards are impossible to copy) as well as 'electronic purse' facilities which could deal the final blow to the inconvenience of having to carry cash.

(Stage 3: Resolution of the problem)

So how do we create a culture which maximises the encouragement given to successful innovation?

Nobody can accurately predict every time whether an innovation will be successful, but we can maximise the number of times we get it right by following two fundamental, related rules.

The first is that when we assess a new technology,we must do everything to avoid getting carried away by enthusiasm for the technology rather than for the potential it offers to the consumer. By putting the consumers' needs of convenience, comfort and security at the heart of our analysis, we can to a large extent ensure that a fascination for technology for technology's sake does not lead us onto the shifting sands of enthusiasm for an impractical technology: that is, one which lacks a viable application.

The second rule is that we must be hard-headed in our approach to analysing the benefits and prospects of a new technology, and under no circumstances indulge in the kind of wordy, jargonesque analyses which are regretfully so common in the reports and assessments of many management consultants.

So much of management consultancy basically amounts to speculative ideas generated by people who usually do not have to bear the consequences of implementing those ideas. Ultimately someone whose own money is at stake – and who adopts an aggressive, down-to-earth, consumer-focused approach to assessing a technological innovation – is far more likely to arrive at a correct conclusion than a business-school trained management consultant who believes that abstract thought and the use of MBA jargon somehow give one's judgements a kind of intrinsic reliability.

-ends-

The letter to the editor

■ ■ ■

Purpose

A letter written, for publication, to the editor of a newspaper or journal your organisation's or client's existing and potential customers are likely to be read can be a surprisingly powerful publicity tool. Coverage is free; indeed, some newspapers or journals even give prizes or small cash sums for the letters. But you don't write the letter to gain these benefits: you do so for the publicity value, which can be considerable.

Not only are you able to attach your name and the name of your organisation to the end of the letter, but the letter will not be published unless you do: newspaper and journals do not publish anonymous letters.

The kind of letters to editors that I am talking about here are not the ones you write to your local paper to protest about lack of progress in constructing a new by-pass, but letters you write or ghost-write on behalf of your organisation or client, in order to advance their interests.

Of course, if you are ghost-writing the letter, the person on whose behalf you are writing must fully approve of the idea, and should sign it. Forging a letter is a criminal offence.

Typical readership

This will be the readership of the newspaper or journal to which you are sending the letter.

What you need to know about the product and/or organisation

You need to know enough about the product and/or organisation you are promoting in order to be aware of a possible viewpoint you could adopt in an ongoing correspondence, or in a response to an item that appeared in the paper.

Blueprint

The secret of writing letters to editors is to keep the letters **short**, **to the point** and **logical**.

The letter must be short – probably no more than about 200 words. Otherwise it runs the risk of being severely cut by the sub-editor, or not used at all.

The letter must be to the point. There is not room for a single word that is not strictly relevant to what you want to say.

The letter must be logical. It must make sense all the way through, and should not contain any unsupported assertions or claims.

As far as the actual structure of your letter to the editor is concerned, I do not wish to be overly dogmatic about how you should build your paragraphs. However, I believe there is a strong case for using the same three-stage construction I suggested for a full-length thoughtpiece article, albeit on a greatly reduced scale.

In other words, your letter should have the following structure:

Stage 1: Statement of the problem

Stage 2: Elaboration of the problem

Stage 3: Resolution of the problem.

I suggest the first stage should consist of one paragraph, the second stage of one or two paragraphs, and the third stage of one paragraph. In the first paragraph you should refer to the date of the letter or coverage in the newspaper or journal to which your own letter relates.

Put your address at the top of the letter (or write on your organisation's or client's letterhead) and write 'FOR PUBLICATION' below this, in order to make clear this letter is indeed for publication, and not just a personal quibble you want to take up with the editor.

Keep the tone of the letter factual and sober at all times.

Which is not to say you can't inject some wit into the letter, because you can.

✍ **EXAMPLE 28**

Wrigley's Wristpads Ltd
High Street
Watford
Herts
WD1 1XX

September 2 1995

FOR PUBLICATION

Dear Sir

I note that in his article 'Repetitive Strain Injury turns writer into dictator' (August 29) your correspondent Michael Smith relates the sad story of William Jones, the novelist who has been forced by Repetitive Strain Injury (RSI) to dictate his work to a secretary, in order to give his painful right arm a chance to heal.

I can well appreciate that the inconvenience and added expense of dictating one's work to a third party – quite apart from the loss of creative spontaneity this entails – must be a serious drawback to any writer. May I mention that the experience of my own organisation – which manufactures and sells a popular brand of wristpad – is that a substantial proportion of cases of RSI arise because the writer's wrist, during work, has nowhere to rest but on the desk in front of the keyboard. The result is the wrist being held in a skewed, unnatural position, with consequent neural (and often muscular) damage to the entire arm.

The use of a wristpad – a firm, bar-shaped cushion which goes on the desk in front of the keyboard and provides the requisite support – can often be extraordinarily beneficial in curing the problem.

I do not, of course, know whether Mr Jones' own difficulty would be amenable to this solution, but if he would care to contact me, I will send him one of our wristpads, with our compliments. It would be most pleasing to know that our product had prevented a writer of his calibre from having to live in a totalitarian state.

119

Your sincerely
John A. Wrigley
Managing Director

KEY LEARNING POINTS

- ■ Try to imagine yourself in your reader's shoes.

- ■ The press release:
  - – The first paragraph must grab the editor's attention.
  - – Keep it newsworthy, short and to the point.

- ■ The 'thoughtpiece' article:
  - – Not an advertisement for your company's products or services.
  - – Must be clear and logical.
  - – Must have an arresting start.

- ■ The letter to the editor:
  - – Can be a powerful publicity tool.
  - – Keep it short, logical and to the point.

5
∎ ∎ ∎

Writing business literature

Corporate brochure

■ ■ ■

Purpose

The purpose of a corporate brochure is to provide a written introduction to the activities and structure of an organisation.

Typical readership

This will naturally depend on to whom your organisation or client wishes to send the brochure.

Of course, just because someone is *sent* a corporate brochure does not mean they will necessarily read it. They will only do so if they find it interesting, and relevant to their needs.

What you need to know about the product and/or organisation

To write a corporate brochure you need to know as much as you can reasonably find out about the organisation, particularly in terms of its unique selling points (USPs): that is, the special advantages it can offer the market compared to these its rivals are able to offer.

Blueprint

The enormous range of the possible configurations a corporate brochure can take, and the variety of its possible contents, make it impossible to suggest a specific blueprint. However, it must, at a minimum, contain all the following information:

- The name of the organisation and its contact details (i.e. address, phone, fax numbers and other information on how to contact the organisation).
- A clear summary of the nature of the organisation's business.
- A detailed, concise account of what the organisation offers its clients or customers.
- Some historical information about how the organisation has developed, so that readers can get a perspective on how it has achieved its success.

- Some details of the 'corporate philosophy' which has made the organisation successful. Don't overdo this, though.

- Information about the organisation's customers and what the organisation does for them. You *must* obtain the customers' permission before mentioning them: neglecting to do this is likely seriously to jeopardise the organisation's relationship with its customer, and could even involve legal problems if the work the organisation is undertaking for the customer is supposed to be confidential.

Avoid boastful accounts of the work the organisation has done for its customers; these will irritate your readers. It is far better to understate the strength of the organisation's relationships with its customers than overstate them.

One of the best ways to include information about the relationship between the organisation and its customers is in the form of quoted testimonials. These do not need to be lengthy; indeed, a succinct one or two sentence quotation can often be more effective than several paragraphs in conveying the message that the customer has benefited considerably from the relationship with the organisation.

123

✍ EXAMPLE 29

The following example is a corporate brochure I wrote on behalf of the information technology consultancy IDOM Consultants S.A. in conjunction with IDOM director John Dembitz. To convey the appearance of the finished brochure, the document is reproduced as it was printed, although without the colour.

Note, how, in this brochure, the descriptive text is written in a sober, factual way, and how the quotations from satisfied customers complement the descriptive text without ever being intrusive or appearing conceited.

Managing change

Deloitte Touche
Tohmatsu
International

Contents

IDOM Consultants is a dynamic and results-orientated information technology (I.T.) consultancy. Founded in 1988 in Geneva, Switzerland, IDOM has built up a reputation for consistently giving its clients the conceptual and practical know-how which they require in order to succeed. This brochure explains IDOM's origins, its achievements to date and its future plans.

Introduction

Origins

The political and economic changes that swept through Central and Eastern Europe in the late-1980s created diversified, competitive markets where previously there had only been planned economies. Central and Eastern European banking infrastructures, designed as they were for operation in a planned economy, needed to be reformed as a matter of urgency. IDOM set out to assist Central and Eastern European banks with this restructuring.

The first country to reorganise its banking structure was Hungary. Working in conjunction with the World Bank, Hungary introduced a 'two-tiered' banking system on January 1 1987.

IDOM's initial mandate was with the Hungarian Foreign Trade Bank to computerise the bank's operational procedures and methodologies.

Within twelve months, IDOM was providing a similar service to several other Hungarian banks. By 1990, IDOM grew to become the market leader in supplying consultancy services to the Hungarian banking sector.

IDOM's Geographical Expansion

Other Central and Eastern European countries needed to modify their banking infrastructures as urgently as Hungarian banks did. By the end of 1990, IDOM was working with banks in former Czechoslovakia (now the Czech and Slovak Republics) and in Poland. The consultancy has continued its expansion in Central and Eastern Europe and is now active throughout the region. IDOM also established subsidiaries in North America (IDOM Inc) and the UK, and has developed a presence in Australasia.

There are three main reasons for IDOM's continued success in the face of increased competition.

1) IDOM has from the outset imposed a rigorous policy of recruiting experienced Western bankers (often with extensive additional I.T. expertise) and training them to be consultants, rather than vice versa.

2) Through local management IDOM has always striven to build real, in-depth knowledge of local market conditions.

3) IDOM provides a practical, hands-on, results-orientated service that gets the job done in an agreed timeframe and within agreed budgetary constraints.

Merger with Deloitte Touche Tohmatsu International

By 1993, IDOM had grown into a successful, diversified, international I.T. consultancy. That same year, IDOM merged with Deloitte Touche Tohmatsu International, one of the world's largest accountancy and management consultancy groups. The terms of the merger position IDOM as Deloitte Touche's I.T. spearhead essentially in Central and Eastern Europe.

IDOM's Expansion to other Business Areas

While continuing the geographical expansion of its banking consultancy services, IDOM has also expanded into other commercial and industrial sectors. This brochure looks at all of IDOM's activities.

Banking consultancy

IDOM's Methodology
IDOM has developed a rigorous, but not inflexible,
eight stage methodology for building a market economy
I.T. structure and operational platform for Central and East
European banks.

IDOM's Methodology
IDOM has developed a rigorous, but not inflexible,
eight stage methodology for building a market economy
I.T. structure and operational platform for Central and East
European banks.

1.

ANALYSIS OF STRATEGIC REQUIREMENTS.

2.

ORGANISATIONAL AND STRUCTURAL

ANALYSIS AND PLANNING.

3.

I.T. PLANNING

4.

NEW SYSTEM PROJECT PLANNING.

5.

CREDIT MANAGEMENT PROCEDURES.

6.

TREASURY AND LIABILITY MANAGEMENT PROCEDURES.

7.

MANAGEMENT INFORMATION SYSTEMS (MIS)

8.

INTERNAL AUDIT PROCEDURES.

This eight-stage methodology is only the starting-point.
IDOM always tailors the methodology to the specific needs
of the client, aimed at achieving efficient and cost-effective
restructuring of the bank. In turn the bank should be able to
obtain competitive advantage and deliver higher profits.

IDOM's Independence

IDOM offers a results-orientated banking consultancy service that is independent of hardware and software system vendors. IDOM's clients have the full confidence that IDOM will survey the range of available technology and software solutions in order to locate the technology and solutions that are most appropriate for the bank's requirements; and which fit within the bank's budget.

The Pressure for Change within the Banking Sector

As a result of the political and economic changes in Central and Eastern Europe, banks in the region found themselves in a market economy where market forces, not the dictates of a central planning office, would decide how resources should be allocated.

The banking infrastructures which had been developed for the region's planned economies were no longer suitable. Furthermore, the planned economies within which Central and East European banks formerly operated did not require these institutions to implement the tried and tested banking principles accepted by this industry throughout the world.

IDOM's Role

IDOM believes that Central and Eastern European banks cannot expect to make the most of the opportunities that exist in the new market economies without expert assistance and advice from a consultancy that understands the nature of the challenges. In particular, IDOM believes that banks in Central and Eastern Europe need the assistance of a consultancy whose consultants are themselves bankers with hands-on experience of the practice of banking. IDOM priviledges the implementation of modern banking systems as an important factor in modernising each bank.

"As our banking system
consultant IDOM has
consistently provided
a quality of service
that was beyond our
expectations; there is
no doubt that these
consultants being
experienced bankers
as well as system specialists were
decisive in
implementing for
Inter-Európa Bank
one of the most
sophisticated bank
information systems in
Eastern-Europe. "

György Iványi
Chairman, Inter-Európa Bank

Manufacturing, Distribution and Finance

IDOM and BPCS

Central and Eastern Europe's industrial sector has also been involved in a process of increasingly rapid restructuring. In 1992, IDOM decided to expand into integrated systems for Manufacturing, Distribution and Finance (MDF) applications. The consultancy's established I.T. expertise - particularly in the implementation of packaged systems - was the spur to this decision.

BPCS - designed and developed by System Software Associates (SSA) - is a leading worldwide integrated MDF package. IDOM's decision to work with SSA was based on a detailed examination of BPCS and on the conclusion that the package had a unique range of functionality and embodied good business practice.

In 1992, IDOM became an affiliate of SSA. IDOM has now set up a separate division - IDOM.MDF - to cater to the needs of industrial clients.

IDOM has already built up considerable experience in implementing BPCS to handle the MDF-related challenges of Central and Eastern European businesses.

BPCS is now available in the most widely-spoken languages of Central and Eastern Europe.

Activities of IDOM.MDF

IDOM.MDF has successfully managed numerous BPCS implementations across a wide range of industries and for clients who range in size from multinationals to small, local firms. Among IDOM.MDF's clients are the Czech Republic, Hungarian and Polish subsidiaries of leading chemical group CIBA-GEIGY.

SSA has a 'client first' philosophy which puts a priority on client success. This fully corresponds with IDOM's own approach to business.

4

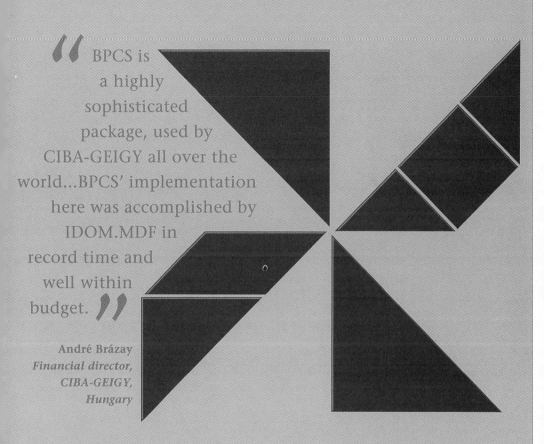

"BPCS is a highly sophisticated package, used by CIBA-GEIGY all over the world...BPCS' implementation here was accomplished by IDOM.MDF in record time and well within budget."

André Brázay
Financial director,
CIBA-GEIGY,
Hungary

Government Institutions

Ministry of Welfare - Hungary
IDOM has co-ordinated the Ministry's office automation system and has provided in-depth information technology consultancy to the Ministry for a system - known as the Medicine Card project - which allows the monitoring and control of patients' consumption of prescribed medicine and their take-up of available subsidies. The new system operates by means of a personal memory card which can be written and read electronically.

Hospitál Péterfy Sándor - Hungary
IDOM participated in the evaluation of proposals to develop a comprehensive and integrated medical data management system for the hospital. IDOM's consultants reviewed the computerisation plans for data maintenance, and assisted the hospital's experts to specify the proposal which gave the best response to the hospital's requirements and which offered the best prospects for maximising health care quality.

I.T. in the Public Sector

Central and local government bodies represent a particularly demanding challenge for I.T. consultancies. The public sector has a duty to taxpayers to obtain maximum value for money on I.T. spend. There is also considerable potential for I.T. to play an essential role in the development of public sector infrastructures which will greatly contribute to a country's overall efficiency and prosperity.

The role of I.T. in enabling the modification and development of government infrastructures is as crucial for central and local government administrative bodies as it is for government-sponsored institutions such as hospitals and other public amenities.

IDOM's Work in the Public Sector

IDOM offers its public sector clients the benefits of in-depth knowledge of how I.T. can be applied to resolve complex issues. As well as this, IDOM's public sector clients enjoy the confidence that the consultancy's strict independence means that its solutions are based on the client's requirements.

IDOM particularly believes that careful planning of an I.T. initiative is the key to how governments can gain maximum benefit from the initiative and gain control over related costs.

IDOM and the Central and Eastern European Public Sector

IDOM has particular expertise in providing I.T. consultancy services to the Central and Eastern European public sector.

Within this sector, the pace of change - and the consequent burdens on government bodies and institutions - is very great. In many cases, I.T. is the only efficient way of developing infrastructures to handle change.

Yet I.T. can never achieve its full potential as a tool for creating new, more effective infrastructures unless it is implemented by experts who have extensive experience of similar I.T. projects, both at the conceptual and practical level.

IDOM's consultants have that experience. The consultancy has successfully completed several I.T. consulting projects for the Central and Eastern European public sector.

 " ...the most important task is to define the objectives
and to implement the selected systems. We decided to
appoint IDOM to perform these tasks as its consultants have
obtained the necessary relevant experience over the course
of the past few years. "

Dr András Jávor
Secretary of State, Ministry of Welfare, Hungary

Software house

In addition to its activities as an I.T. consultancy, IDOM offers a full bespoke software development service.

This service is wide in its remit; covering selection and customisation to clients' needs of an external package as well as development of bespoke software.

In its role as a software house, IDOM brings to the task of software specification, design, building and implementation the same disciplines as in its I.T. consultancy.

IDOM's Software Development Methodology

Central to IDOM's success as a software house is its software development methodology. Like all of IDOM's methodologies, this is rigorous, but not inflexible. The decisive factor governing the precise nature of the methodology is the clients' needs.

The software development methodology usually covers the following stages:

- initial discussion of client's specific requirements
- production of recommendations for the best way to solve the clients' problems

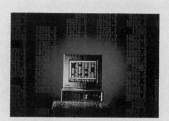

- if a packaged software solution is chosen:
  - the evaluation of relevant packages
  - selection of the most suitable package
  - customisation of package to specific client requirements
- if a bespoke software solution is chosen:
  - the full project management of customised software design development
  - design and building of all software;
  - preliminary and final testing of software
  - implementation of software;
  - full post-implementation support.

IDOM's ten step approach to software development

1.
FUNCTIONAL ANALYSIS (FA)

Development of a logical data model and the external specification of the user interface.

2.
APPROVAL OF THE FA DOCUMENTATION

FA documentation reconciliation with users.

3.
SYSTEM PLANNING

The plan of the implementation of the functionalities included in the FA, CASE-METHOD.

4.
DATABASE DESIGN

The physical data model will be created in order to produce database tables.

5.
PROGRAM DESIGN

Detailed specification of the program modules using CASE tools for 4GL programs.

6.
PROGRAMMING

The generation of software modules specified with any other sophisticated language.

7.
MIGRATION

Planned import of data from the old system.

8.
ACCEPTANCE TESTING, TRAINING

To check the reliability and the adequacy of the application software, simulating live operations is an essential pre-requisite for starting the new system.

9.
DOCUMENTATION

Production of full documentation for the application software, and the user manuals.

10.
ACCEPTANCE OF THE SYSTEM FOR LIVE RUNNING

Final hardware and software installation and the start of daily operations on the new system.

“ We selected IDOM as our long term
strategic partner for the design and
development of our bespoke software
requirements, and their maintenance, given
IDOM's proven capability to effectively
control quality, and consistently deliver
on schedule. ”

Dr Péter Póka
IT Director, Magyar Külkereskedelmi Bank

Training

IDOM *BPP*
BANK TRAINING

Origin

Assisting clients with their training requirements is an integral part of IDOM's activities. The very nature of IDOM's consultancy means that IDOM consultants work side-by-side with client staff. The skills transfer which occurs in this situation is the genesis of IDOM's work in the area of training. IDOM has particular expertise in training Central and Eastern European banking staff in good banking practice. Training extends to banking disciplines as diverse as credit control, treasury management, internal audit, etc. Implementation of integrated banking systems provides an ideal platform for such training, the transfer of know how related to contemporary banking operations, products and services.

Joint Venture with BPP plc

In 1992, in response to client demands for more formalised training programmes, IDOM entered into a 50:50 joint venture with BPP Holdings plc, the largest publicly quoted training company in the UK. Based in Budapest, the joint venture is known as IDOM-BPP Kft.

IDOM-BPP's Training Services

These cover three principal areas:
• training for individual client organisations
• training courses open to all
• publication of training material

Individual clients' training needs vary considerably. For example, one client may simply wish to define the precise nature of its overall training requirements. IDOM has assisted several clients - including the Polish Ministry of Finance - with precisely this task. Another client may have a requirement for training a substantial number of employees. Yet another may require support with creating a human resource department and defining a career development program.

The second area of IDOM-BPP's training activity is the provision of training courses open to all. From its Budapest base, IDOM-BPP is able to provide to Central and Eastern European banks more than 40 bank training courses in almost every field of banking.

The third area of IDOM-BPP's training activity consists of the provision of published training material. IDOM-BPP provides a series of self-study and reference handbooks which meet the training needs of Central and Eastern European banks today, and which will continue to meet the changing training needs of banks in the future.

// I am pleased we selected IDOM for
this project, and I am very impressed with the professional
approach of your consultants. We certainly want to retain you
for the implementation phase and wish to maintain an ongoing relationship with you. I believe we may require your
assistance on other projects in the future **//**

Wolfgang Bauer
Creditanstalt Investment Bank, Warsaw

// We had a tight, demanding time-table
to start-up a new bank. IDOM's professionalism, it's
expertise, experience, independence and high calibre
people, helped us find the right I.T. solution from a
difficult and pressure laden situation. Our bank now
considers IDOM an important external resource. **//**

Dariusz Ledworowski
President, Bank Rolno Przemyslowy S.A.

// IDOM have given a great deal of
help to Bank Staropolski in the process
of selection of banking software systems
and in founding information strategy
for the Bank. The cooperation is going
very well and it will be continuing
during the implementation of
the system. **//**

J Barszczewski
President, Bank Staropolski

Designed by Meridian Design Associates +44 81 542 6288

The newsletter

■ ■ ■

Purpose

Whereas the purpose of the corporate brochure is to provide an introduction to the activities and structure of an organisation, the point of a newsletter is to furnish a regular, topical, interesting range of information about the organisation's ongoing activities.

Newsletters can be highly effective as communication tools. Not only do they give the organisation the opportunity to publicise key aspects of its activities, such as new product launches, contract wins, staff changes and new developments in its approach to doing business, but there is also scope for including comments by its senior managers on matters of importance to the industry, as well as features which invite feedback from readers: such as a letters page.

Typical readership

As with the corporate brochure, this will be whoever the organisation chooses it to be.

What you need to know about the product and/or organisation

You can only write a newsletter if you have an in-depth knowledge of major developments at the organisation and of the principal political, regulatory, financial and commercial factors which impinge on it.

In practice, it is unlikely you will know everything it is necessary to know in order to write a well-informed, wide-ranging, in-depth newsletter. The newsletter will probably require you to collaborate with other people in the organisation. I have found the best way of handling this is to obtain drafts of material – or even bare notes or lists of bullet points – from people at the organisation who have the requisite knowledge, and to base written material on these. Even when you are given a complete, well-written piece of text on which to base material, it is important you ensure that the style and approach it uses is consistent with the rest of the material. A newsletter needs an editor, and one of the primary functions of the editor is to harmonise the style, all the way through.

Blueprint

As with the corporate brochure, the possible range and scope of a corporate newsletter is too broad for there to be any sense in suggesting an all-encompassing blueprint for it. However, certain key points can nonetheless be made about the contents of the newsletter.

The first and most fundamental decision you need to make – as with all marketing copy – relates to the precise nature of the newsletter's readership. Is your newsletter designed to be read by the organisation's customers or its staff? If it is an *external* newsletter (i.e. one designed to be read by the organisation's customers), it will require more formality, both in terms of overall tone and contents, than an *in-house* newsletter.

141

The general characteristics of each type of newsletter are as follows:

External newsletter

- Serious in tone and content.
- Should primarily contain information the customer is likely to find of practical benefit (e.g. relating to products and services supplied by the organisation).
- Scope for containing comment (perhaps attributed to a senior person at the organisation) on general matters of industry interest.
- Information about staff should, generally, be limited to recruitment information and changes in responsibilities of staff who are directly serving customer needs. New telephone numbers of staff whose responsibilities are changing, or who are starting work at the organisation, should always be given.
- Can contain corporate information (e.g. details of new contract wins, and so on), but not too much of this. The readership of an external newsletter should *not* be seen as a captive audience for being bombarded with information

that is primarily of interest to the organisation rather than its customers.

■ Scope for including interactive features such as a letters' page or a forum for answering readers' queries (e.g. those relating to the organisation's products and services). If an interactive feature is included, it should be conducted with professionalism and a certain gravity: ultimately the people who are writing in are customers and must be treated with respect. You *must* answer all queries and letters, even the ones you decide not to publish.

In-house newsletter

■ Can be less serious in tone and content.

■ Should contain information which helps to give readers the exciting sense of being part of a strong community.

■ Scope for containing detailed information about staff and staff events. This can be chatty, but be careful not to cross the line between being chatty and being patronising.

■ Possibility of including interactive features: e.g. quizzes, competitions, crosswords etc. If these *are* included, they should be of a high standard: just because this is an in-house newsletter doesn't mean there is any room for third-rate material in it.

Whichever type of newsletter it is, you must decide on an *editorial format* for it. This is a blueprint each issue of the newsletter should follow in order to be consistent and to have maximum impact. There is no reason why you need to feel hidebound by the format; indeed, if it is unduly restrictive it won't be much use to you; but readers are generally happier with a newsletter when they know roughly what they are likely to find in it. The use of an editorial format also makes the newsletter much easier to prepare and write.

Other important points to make about newsletters are:

The title

If you are taking over the writing of a newsletter which has already been going for some time, the title of the newsletter will probably be something you inherit.

If this is not the case, or if you are starting a newsletter from scratch, you may have the opportunity to choose a title, or make suggestions for it. Take care over this choice, as it can play a crucial role in the success of the newsletter. Avoid obviously 'clever' titles. Instead, for an external newsletter try to think of a title which summarises the organisation's overall commercial activity, and for an in-house newsletter select a 'friendly' title which conveys the idea of communication between the organisation and its staff.

I have titled two newsletters during the past year: *Contact*, the newsletter of Datastream Investment Management Services, an organisation which specialises in providing computer-based investment administration information (the 'contact' is the contact between the user and the information) and *In Touch*, the in-house newsletter of the IDOM Group.

143

Editorial protocols

You must be consistent in editorial matters; not only throughout an issue of the newsletter but also in successive issues. The only reliable way of achieving this is to make certain decisions about editorial protocols in advance and stick to them.

The types of decisions you will need to make concern such issues as:

- Whether to write 'percent', 'per cent' or '%'.
- What your standardised spelling should be of words which can be written with a hyphen, with both words together, or separately.
- How to write the name of the organisation and its products or services: this may seem obvious, but often you will want to use a shortened form of names, or an acronym, and you need to standardise your usage. Remember, too, that names of organisations should be treated grammatically as being third person singular and not first person plural.

✍ EXAMPLE 30

This example gives the full editorial text of a recent edition of *The Custodian*, the newsletter of the London-based global custody organisation Barclays Global Securities Services. I have written this newsletter since spring 1994.

This is an external newsletter aimed at highly-educated professionals in the banking sector. The newsletter must therefore speak their language, focus on matters which they are likely to find of importance, and above all never 'talk down' to them.

The editorial format for the newsletter is as follows:

Front Page: Title, general industry thoughtpiece *or* major product story, list of contents.

Page Two: Continuation of front page story, second leading article.

Pages Three and Four: Coverage of major developments in the securities industry, around the world.

Page Five: Major corporate news story.

Page Six: Other corporate news stories.

In the following example I have preserved the paragraphing style of *The Custodian*, which is to indent new paragraphs without leaving a space after the previous paragraph. While this is not the paragraphing style used in this book, it is the preferable style for newsletters, as it makes them resemble newspapers.

Note, too, the use of the square brackets in the newsletter text to contain instructions to the printer that should not form part of the actual copy.

COPY FOR 'THE CUSTODIAN'

SUMMER 1995 ISSUE   145

Requires full approval by Barclays Global Securities Services

Final Draft

(Please note: in the following text, square brackets [...] are used to indicate production instructions that should not appear in the copy.

Underlining signifies italic script).

[FRONT PAGE]

Issue Fifteen   Summer 1995

THE CUSTODIAN

Barclays Global Securities Services News

[CONTENTS PANEL]

CONTENTS

Featuring: United Kingdom, Ecuador, Indonesia, Malaysia, Australia, The Netherlands, Italy

[FRONT PAGE STORY]

Barclays **Infoshare**<u>Online</u> Service Goes Global

by Don Harrington

146

Increasingly all major global custodians are coming to accept that excellence in the provision of basic custody services will be taken for granted by clients, and that if the custodian is to establish a real competitive edge it must excel in the quality of the value-added services it provides.

In today's highly competitive custody industry, value-added services such as stock lending, tax reclamation, contractual settlement and performance measurement are increasingly in demand. Nor do clients' requirements stop there; clients continue to expect custodians to provide an ever expanding range of trust and portfolio administration services.

As further evidence of its dynamic approach to responding to these demands, Barclays has made the radical decision to widen the range of investment and performance services it supplies under the Infoshare brand name.

The **Infoshare** product has been servicing a largely US-based range of clients for many years. Barclays' ever-diversifying and innovative client base means that an essential part of Barclays' overall business strategy must be to develop and deliver increasingly sophisticated products. Barclays has created **Infoshare**<u>Online</u> to meet client demands.

Key Trends

Two major trends are driving the changes in what Barclays' clients expect from investment administration.

Firstly, an increasing number of fund trustees are appointing multiple managers. Secondly, in-house managed funds wish to outsource an increasing proportion of their administration services.

The first trend is driven by the fund manager's desire to gain the benefits of risk diversification, combined with a desire to appoint the best specialised managers available. The trend is furthered by the increasing use of innovative fund structure techniques such as Common Investment Funds (CIF).

The second trend is driven partly by the cost and timescale involved when investment in new technology takes place, and partly by a perceived need on the part of fund management organisations to concentrate on managing assets rather than managing administration. This applies as much to an in-house managed pension or insurance fund as to independent investment management organisations.

Product Elements

A key feature of a first-class asset servicing function is that it remains sufficiently flexible to be able to react to a changing market and to changing client demand without needing radically to rebuild its capability. In meeting this need, Barclays has recognised a number of key product areas which are common to many clients while being able to tailor these or other services to meet specific client requirements. These are:

Investment Accounting

Most funds account on a monthly basis and require a full set of audited investment accounts, including full cash, asset and income reconciliations delivered in a timely fashion, and at a standard of presentation which does not require further presentation. This is precisely what the service offers.

Trustee Monitoring

Fund trustees are constantly under pressure to monitor fund activity for increasingly sophisticated investment mandates, and to ensure that funds comply with a relentless regulatory environment. The service meets regulatory requirements in full.

Fund Administration

The drive by funds to diversify the investment mandates and to structure portfolios to take advantage of the most advantageous fiscal frameworks available make the administrator's task increasingly diffi-

147

cult. Flexible systems capable of almost endless options for consolidation and 'look through' accounting are required to cater for these needs. This flexibility is a key part of the service.

Master Custody

Barclays recognises that some of its clients wish to retain several custodial relationships and therefore require a consolidated master custodian/master record-keeper service. Barclays has therefore established a full SWIFT format messaging capability to link with other custodians.

Performance Measurement

Portfolio diversification is an important method for maximising return and minimising risk. In order for this technique to work properly, plan sponsors must be able to monitor investment return on this initial level of asset allocation in order to ensure that the diversification chosen will yield a maximum return for beneficiaries. Plan sponsors must also be able to monitor the individual mandates against appropriate benchmarks to ensure that the chosen manager is truly the 'best of breed'.

In addition to providing its own performance measurement service, Barclays is also happy to link with other service providers if its clients wish for this.

Investment Support

A key requirement of an investment support function is to provide rapid analysis of where the portfolio is today and to provide the analysis required to achieve a detailed final objective. Sophisticated analysis tools coupled with ease of integration into modern Windows-based applications are required in order to achieve these objectives. The service provides the precise levels of investment support required.

[PAGE TWO]

The Barclays Response – **Infoshare**Online

The **Infoshare** product range is supported out of Barclays' New York office, backed by a local support centre in the UK. **Infoshare** provides a full investment accounting service, including truly independent reconciliation against custodians. It is in effect a back office outsourcing service which maintains the client's accounting ledgers, *whether or not the assets are in Barclays' own custody*.

The base accounting function offers an International Accounting

Standards (GAAP) compliant service with a vast range of full multi-currency accounting options: such as average cost, lifo, fifo and specific lot. The multi-currency environment which operates at an individual transaction level uses the WM/Reuters 4.00pm London benchmark exchange rates. Market information and prices are taken from Barclays' own databases, EXTEL, IDSI, Bloomberg, Reuters, Valorinform and a network of brokers worldwide.

The Investment Administration function is front-ended by a market-leading technology – **Infoshare**Online, which is a Windows-compliant local personal computer (PC) database which enables Barclays to deliver accounting and performance data, along with an asset database, including price history, locally to clients' offices. This database is supplemented by a user-friendly request facility which enables Barclays' clients to access its mainframe computers to request specific reports, customised to their requirements.

The local PC environment provides a vast array of analytical functionality as well as an almost endless range of reporting capabilities. If preferred full integration with other Windows-compliant spreadsheet or report writers can also be provided.

149

The Barclays Advantage

By siting its investment administration function in New York, Barclays' has ensured that its clients can take advantage of the world's time zones to ensure that the service fully reflects trading and settlement activity around the world.

Assuming that timely instructions are received from Barclays' clients, the investment information can be delivered to clients worldwide as they arrive in their offices. Price feeds are taken as each market closes; this allows Barclays to revalue assets at the earliest opportunity. Highly automated electronic links with the custody environment enable Barclays to deliver the results of the accounting process to clients at a time when they are most in need of it. This enables Barclays to offer a real competitive edge to its clients.

By establishing the investment administration function outside its custody operations, Barclays can offer a truly independent service for administering its clients' accounting ledgers, whether or not Barclays is the custodian for these assets.

The only effective way to gauge the flexibility, adaptability and quality of presentation which this market-leading application offers is to see it in action. Barclays cordially invites its clients to arrange a demonstration through their relationship manager.

The Struggle to Find the Best Sub-Custodians

by Keith Norris

How is Barclays able to be certain that the sub-custodians (agent banks) with which it chooses to work are the best available in the marketplace?

Some clients might imagine that with one of the world's largest proprietary networks of offices, Barclays does not need to maintain constant vigilance over the quality of the service provided by its own offices.

Barclays believes, however, that the only way to ensure a successful and reliable network is to use the best service providers in each market. This policy has meant that on three occasions over the last two years, the decision has been made to move the custody function from a Barclays office to an external sub-custodian.

Of course, the overall standard of the Barclays global network of proprietary offices is extremely high; the decision not to use one of its own offices is only taken after a careful evaluation of the situation and the alternatives. However, Barclays firmly believes that no global custodian whose worldwide client base includes hundreds of the world's leading institutional investors can afford to rest on its laurels.

Whether the external sub-custodian is needed to replace a Barclays office that has been found wanting or because Barclays wishes to establish a service base in an emerging market where it does not already have a presence, the selection process is extremely rigorous. Within the global custody industry Barclays is renowned for the close scrutiny it employs when selecting a sub-custodian. Several other major custodians have adopted selection procedures similar to those which Barclays pioneered.

The first stage of the Barclays sub-custodian selection process is always to consult Barclays internal research service, which provides key information on the major banks in whichever country Barclays is considering appointing a custodian. This information ranges over such matters as creditworthiness, market information, the names of the major players and those of the best providers.

Once this information has been analysed, a list of potential providers will emerge. Barclays will send shortlisted participants two separate questionnaires; one questionnaire focuses on *safekeeping*, the other on overall levels of *service*.

There is nothing haphazard about how these questionnaires are compiled and how the responses are assessed. The questionnaires represent the fruit of literally hundreds of man-years of practical experience of working with sub-custodians and knowledge of client requirements.

The responses are assessed according to a complex, systematic scoring system which enables a high level of objective judgement to be applied. The point is that no matter how enthusiastic, dynamic and 'hungry' a sub-custodian might be for Barclays' business, global custody is a methodical, precise service as well as one offering considerable opportunities for personal flair. If the fundamentals of service aren't in place at the prospective sub-custodian, no amount of drive and energy will replace this.

Which is not to say that Barclays omits the need to make a more subjective assessment of the sub-custodian *once Barclays is certain the prospective sub-custodian has the requisite fundamentals in place*.

These fundamentals will include, for example: quality of safekeeping facilities, service quality guarantees, effectiveness of in-house protocols and procedures, price, technological facilities, skills and qualifications of personnel, linguistic abilities of personnel, speed of answering the telephone, quality of references, standard and appearance of reports, security and confidentiality guarantees.

More subjective factors which will subsequently be addressed if the candidate passes the hurdle of the fundamentals would include: appearance of offices (Barclays' assessors insist on visiting the offices where the custody work will take place, not merely the plush boardroom used for meetings), the value that can be added by the quality of the relationship and responsiveness to queries.

Nor is the selection process over once the decision is made. For Barclays, the monitoring of its agent banks – whether they are its own proprietary offices or externally appointed custodians – is an ongoing process.

Finally, where an emerging market is concerned, Barclays may make the decision not to appoint an agent bank at all if the legal and regulatory framework is insufficiently developed to enable good title to be gained, maintained and exchanged with certainty.

We are not interested in providing a global custody service for its own sake. We need to feel comfortable that we can provide the same high level of service in an emerging market we provide throughout our network. However, if the conditions in an emerging market are, in our judgement, still too difficult for us to be comfortable there, we may lobby at several levels within the market, with the aim of modifying and improving the conditions. Ultimately we are committed to being a truly worldwide global custodian. This includes those markets that look on the face of it difficult or impossible to enter safely.

[PAGES THREE AND FOUR]

AROUND THE WORLD

United Kingdom

Settlement performance by the securities industry since five-day rolling settlement was introduced on 26 June 1995 has surpassed even the most optimistic expectations, according to figures released by the London Stock Exchange (LSE).

Since 3 July (the first T+5 settlement day), a daily average of about 88 per cent of bargains by number and about 93 per cent by value have settled on the due date. An average of 29,000 bargains with a value of over £2 billion were recorded each day since T+5 was introduced.

Bernie Till, the LSE's rolling settlement programme manager, told *The Custodian*: "These excellent results have been achieved through the efforts of all industry participants and demonstrate the industry's willingness to attain real improvements in settlement."

Five-day settlement is the second stage in a series of improvements to the UK share settlement system which began in July 1994 when 10-day rolling settlement replaced the 200-year old Account System. Shortening the period between dealing and settlement reduces the risk involved in share transactions and brings the UK closely into line with current international practice.

Christine Dann, director of business operations at the LSE, commented: "The Exchange's success in introducing rolling settlement has triggered a more sweeping settlement improvement during the last year than in the previous two hundred years of Account Settlement. It also demonstrates that the new arrangements accommodate the needs of both the professional and retail investor."

The LSE is also on target to introduce dematerialised stock lending on 29 September 1995. This new service will enable institutions to hold stock positions with the LSE's central nominee name in paperless form, thus achieving book entry settlement of stock loans and market bargains.

Ecuador

In a move which represents yet another step in its expansion into emerging markets, Barclays has launched a 17f-5 sub-custody service in Ecuador.

Ecuador, a Latin American republic bordered by Columbia and Peru, and with a population of just over eleven million, has a rapidly growing securities market. As one of the last countries in Latin America to modernise and open up its capital markets, Ecuador has – according to a Reuters survey – become one of Latin America's most profitable stock markets for investors, with an average return of 22 per cent in 1994.

An appropriate legal framework for the market has now been established, bringing greater efficiency, transparency and security over the buying and selling of equities and fixed income instruments. Of the 115 companies listed on the two official stock exchanges (located in Quito and Guayaquil), the equity of six companies is actively traded. Local brokers are limited to transactions in listed securities on the exchanges, while the still unregulated OTC market is dominated by financial institutions. Settlement is usually T+2, with a a maximum of T+5 for transactions between the two exchanges.

153

For further information and copies of the Ecuador country summary and foreign investors' documentation package, please contact your relationship manager.

Indonesia

There have been two important procedural changes relating to the imposition of stamp duty in Indonesia.

Firstly, procedures for stamp duty have changed with respect to brokers. Prior to the introduction of automated trading on the Jakarta Stock Exchange on 22 May 1995, brokers issued a separate contract note for each transaction, with every transaction attracting stamp duty at the prevailing rate. Subsequent to the introduction of automated trading, however, on 22 May 1995, brokers no longer issue separate contract notes.

Instead, at the end of the day's two trading sessions on the Stock Exchange, brokers receive a print-out listing all transactions effected during the session. This listing will attract one payment only of stamp duty, at IDR 2000, which brokers absorb. There is therefore no longer any stamp duty charged to brokers' clients in respect of transactions on the Stock Exchange.

Secondly, there is to be a gradual introduction of changes to the registration process in Indonesia, with consequent changes to how stamp duty is imposed.

Under existing procedures, it has not been the practice for registrars – with the exception of just one registrar – to charge stamp duty in respect of shares sent for registration. However, registrars now require that the registration form which accompanies new-style share certificates sent for registration will be stamped at a flat rate of IDR 2000 per settlement. This charge will be added to Barclays' clients' monthly fee invoices.

Barclays will keep its clients advised of any further developments or changes to the procedures for collecting stamp duty on securities transactions

Malaysia

The Malaysian Central Depository (MCD) has announced a plan to accelerate the conversion process of the companies listed on the Main Board of the Kuala Lumpur Stock Exchange (KLSE).

The plan calls for all new listings on the Main Board to be compulsorily moved into the Central Depository System (CDS) from 1 October 1995.

In a separate development, the KLSE has imposed new rules relating to Board Lots of securities. As from 30 June 1995, Board Lots must constitute a marketable parcel of one thousand (1,000) units of securities in a single certificate only. The Clearing House will reject any delivery of securities which are not in a Board Lot of a single certificate.

Clients with queries about these developments should contact their relationship manager.

Australia

The Australian Stock Exchange (ASX) has decided to defer the start date for Phase 2 of the Clearing House Electronic Sub-Registry System (CHESS) from October 1995 to March 1996.

Phase 2 of CHESS provides 'Delivery Versus Payment' (DVP) settlement for ASX transactions between brokers and institutions, including custodians who are CHESS participants, such as Barclays, based in Sydney.

The ASX said it regretted the need to defer the start of Phase 2, but added it recognised that DVP settlement was a ground-breaking development for the ASX markets and the Australian banking system, and that it was essential all clearing house participants and banks had sufficient time thoroughly to test their systems and procedures.

The deferment will allow participants and banks additional time to prepare for the changeover and takes into account the December 1995/January 1996 holiday season. The additional time will also allow for dress rehearsals involving participants and banks.

There are now more than 440,000 holdings on the CHESS subregister, with these holdings having a market value of some A$128.4 billion: that is, over 40 per cent of the total ASX market capitalisation. About 900 quoted securities have now been converted to CHESS. Transactions in these securities represent more than 75 per cent of the total value of ASX turnover.

The Netherlands

In order to comply with international requirements, the Dutch Central Depository NEGICEF has developed a new method to settle trades in the Netherlands. The new settlement system, known as NECICOM, will provide a delivery versus payment (DVP) facility and therefore offer same-day value.

NECICOM will also alter the way the participants of NECIGEF communicate with one another and with NECIGEF itself. Unlike the current method, whereby a participant settles a trade simply by sending an instruction to NECIGEF to transfer securities from its depot to the depot of another participant, in future trades will only settle provided the two trade instructions match within NECICOM.

For this reason, as well as on account of the reduced settlement cycle (T+3), it is of great importance that instructions are passed on to NECICOM as quickly as possible. As soon as instructions have been received, NECICOM will inform the participant about the status of the trade. In the event that a buy or sell instruction cannot be matched with an instruction from the opposite party, a notification to this effect will be issued by NECICOM.

Barclays Amsterdam has already enhanced its settlement system, Bank/View, in order automatically to pass on all instructions received from Barclays' clients. At the same time, Bank/View will enable Barclays to report automatically on the status of trades, either via the Remote Access Service of Bank/View or via SWIFT messages MT539 and MT534. In other words, Barclays Amsterdam is fully ready for Straight Through Processing (STP) in this respect.

Following a last moment postponement of NECICOM in June

because of problems with the matching criteria and because some banks were not ready for the new settlement system, NECICOM is now expected to go live sometime in the autumn.

Italy

The Italian Stock Exchange CONSOB and the Bank of Italy have issued a joint statement announcing that as from 16 February 1996, month-end settlement will be scrapped in favour of T+5 rolling settlement.

As well as effecting this radical change to the settlement method in Milan, the reform will:

- modify the dividend collection process, as pay date will no longer coincide with the ex date. Pay date will now be about 10 working days after the ex date

- eliminate monthly contango loans (riporti).

Clients seeking clarification of these changes should contact their relationship manager.

[PAGE FIVE]

Barclays Launches New Short-Term Investment Funds

Barclays Global Securities Services, in conjunction with BZW Investment Management (BZWIM) has announced the launch of a new short-term investment fund (STIF) family. The family of funds, which are ideally suited to cash deposits made for between one to three months (although daily deposits are also acceptable) are designed to maximise investor choice, and cover a spectrum of risk profiles from cash deposits to intermediate maturity bonds.

Domiciled in Dublin's International Financial Services Centre, the funds give institutional investors access to a range of funds and markets covering fixed income, global equity indices and actively managed equities.

The first fund in the family to be launched is the BZW Fixed Income Selection Fund plc, listed on the Irish Stock Exchange in Dublin. It is an open-ended investment company with an umbrella-type structure, and offers five actively managed cash and fixed income funds, all of which are AAA credit rated by Moody's. These funds include:

- a sterling fund.

- two US dollar cash funds.

- a sterling short-duration, fully currency-hedged international bond fund.

- a US dollar short-duration, fully currency-hedged international bond fund.

The investment objectives of the funds are to achieve a high degree of capital preservation, together with an income yield equivalent to wholesale money market short-term interest rates. With a minimum investment of £250,000, funds are pooled to provide economies of scale in the accessing of the wholesale money markets together with the important diversification of borrowers, markets and sector risk. The fund is valued and dealt in daily, with the shares' value including income and other profits which are accumulated and rolled up into the fund.

The fund is specially geared to provide investment vehicles for more stable, managed investment type cash looking to maximise its return for a given level of risk.

157

The fund is not liable to Irish Corporation tax, Capital Gains Tax nor any withholding tax. Investors in any doubt about their tax position should take appropriate advice.

Barclays Global Securities Services provides direct access to sub-set funds within the umbrella fund and offers clients the added advantage of the comfort level that comes from being able to do business through their existing custody relationship.

The launch of this new fund makes Barclays one of the few institutions to offer a highly-rated, professionally-managed investment vehicle which will have a wide appeal to investors looking for secure and attractive locations for cash surpluses. Whereas most short-term investment funds are limited in scope, thereby often involving the investor in a relatively high risk, this new family of funds provides an attractive, balanced portfolio.

For further information please contact Andrew Muchall on 0171 699 4304.

[PAGE SIX]

Barclays Wins Three Major New Mandates

Barclays has further demonstrated the scale and success of its new business initiatives by winning three important new mandates. These are:

- Barclays has been awarded a major contract by the international clearing house Cedel to act as its domestic custodian in Hong Kong

- In France, Barclays has been appointed custodian to an investment portfolio of about $125 million managed by Credit Commercial de France. The portfolio covers investments in Italy, Greece, Morocco, Egypt and South Africa.

Final agreement for this mandate came during Barclays' participation in the Interfinances Expobanques exhibition and conference, the largest event of its kind in France.

- In Scotland, Barclays has been appointed independent global custodian to the £450 million Edinburgh-based Plumbing & Mechanical Services (UK) Industry-Wide Pension Scheme.

Barclays Awarded Coveted Industry Quality Standard

Barclays Corporate Trustees, a division of Barclays Global Securities Services (BGSS), has become the first Corporate Trustee to be awarded the ISO9002 certificate of registration by the British Standards Institution (BSI).

The standard ISO9002 is an internationally recognised quality standard awarded by the British Standards Institution to suppliers who meet the necessary benchmark for work processes and service levels. This standard imposes a set of stringent requirements for suppliers to meet, both from an operational and quality standpoint.

Julian Gibbs, a director of Barclays Global Securities Services, commented: "I am delighted that Barclays Corporate Trustees has become the first trustee to have achieved the distinction of receiving ISO9002 registration. In reaching the necessary standard we have demonstrated our commitment to quality and diligence and emphasised our commitment to offer a superior service to our clients."

Barclays Launches New Information Services

As part of its constant drive to supply its clients with the information they need to maximise their competitive impact on the international investment scene, Barclays has enhanced its information services.

In association with the organisation Faxtrans, Barclays has launched a new service to provide a wide range of in-depth country and market-specific information by fax. The information is available on demand by telephone or fax to any client of Barclays.

For further details, please contact your relationship manager or call Andrew Bainbridge on 0171 699 4283.

A *Data Exchange Guide* has been produced to coincide with the move to T+5 settlement at the London Stock Exchange, which advises Barclays' clients of settlement cut-off times for receipt of trade instructions in the UK and all the other markets where Barclays operates.

Please call your relationship manager if you would like a copy of the Data Exchange Guide.

Barclays Appoints Martin Bilham at Trowbridge

Barclays has appointed Martin Bilham as head of operational support at the Barclays network centre in Trowbridge, UK.

Bilham, who took up his new duties on 17 July, brings with him 24 years' experience of the global custody business. He was with Bank of America for two years, Daiwa Europe for five years, and Manufacturers Hanover for 17 years.

Bilham's new responsibilities as head of operational support cover the Information Centre, the provision of Management Information Systems and Control and Audit.

Martin Bilham told *The Custodian*: "I am glad of the opportunity to join a custodian whose energy, resourcefulness, innovativeness and dynamism are unrivalled."

He added: "I see my principal objectives as being to provide a wide range of client and processing facilities to the sales and marketing side of the business, the relationship management teams and the UK and international operations. These facilities will include: a help desk service for clients; a management information environment designed to produce targeted information for operational purposes as well as for front-end sales, marketing and relationship management areas; monitoring of service levels and operational standard; maintenance of all information held within the distributed databases; and development of new clients who are based outside the European timezone."

Barclays Features in Two Leading Industry Publications

Barclays has featured in two major new independent publications for the global custody industry. These are: *Global Securities Services* by Simon Thomas and Simon Murray – an in-depth buyers' guide for institutional funds – which is available for £395 per copy from Thomas Murray Limited, 212 Piccadilly, London W1V 9LD. Tel: +44 171 917

159

2859 and *Global Custody: A Guide for Investors* by James Essinger, available for £350 per copy from Financial Times Management Reports, Maple House, 149 Tottenham Court Road, London W1P 2LL, Tel: +44 171 896 2222.

-ends-

The case study

■ ■ ■

Purpose

The case study is designed to give existing and potential customers, as well as other interested persons (such as journalists) concise, focused information about what the organisation can do for one or more of its customers.

Case studies can be extremely powerful marketing tools. They bring the organisation's activities to life, and act as a reference and testimonial that is vital in both senses of the word.

Typical readership

Again, the organisation has complete freedom of choice in deciding to whom the case study should be sent or distributed.

What you need to know about the product and/or organisation

You need to have a detailed knowledge of what the organisation has done for the customer or customers who are the subject of the case study.

It is often impossible to obtain this information purely from the organisation itself; you will usually have to obtain additional information from the customer: ideally directly from the customer rather than via someone at the organisation, who will inevitably adopt their own view of the supplier/customer relationship.

Blueprint

The key to writing successful case studies is that they should focus on the activities and business needs of the *customer* and detail how the supplier helped to meet those needs, rather than focus primarily on the supplier's activities.

In essence, therefore, the case study should be the story of how the supplier helped to make the customer more successful.

You achieve this effect by telling the story from the customer's point of view. Make sure you have abundant quoted comment in the case study from the customer (I recommend that at least one-quarter of the copy consist of quoted comment) and use bullet-points to emphasise the precise benefits which the supplier has brought to the customer.

There is also scope for including information about the supplier and its products or services, but do this discreetly, throughout the text, rather than in a solid and obvious lump.

✍️ EXAMPLE 31

This example reproduces a case study supplied by banking software house FIserv (Europe) Limited. This case study is well laid out, displays the necessary focus on the customer's needs, makes the customer central to the whole thing, uses extensive and appropriate customer comment, and summarises key benefits by means of bullet points.

161

'**Our ambition is to make**
the focus on customer service
key to everything that we do'

Brunon Bartkiewicz, Vice President, Bank Slaski

A Fiserv (Europe) Ltd case study of Bank Slaski

Fiserv helps Bank Slaski become first in customer banking

The town of Wadowice in the south of Poland is best known as the birthplace of Pope John Paul II. In April 1994 it also witnessed the introduction of cutting edge retail banking technology by Bank Slaski, one of Poland's most progressive banks. The bank selected its Wadowice branch to initiate a highly innovative, IBM AS/400 based, integrated customer banking solution with its strategic partner, Fiserv Europe. The pilot was a major success and has already been followed by the implementation of Fiserv's Comprehensive Banking System (CBS) across the network, including the local Bielsko Biala region, as well as key branches in Krakow and Katowice. The main branch in Katowice has approximately sixty cash/teller positions and is one of the largest of its type in Poland. Work will continue into 1995, but the results are already tangible. Bank Slaski now has a clear advantage over its Polish competitors (many of whom in terms of technology are still at the investigation stage) and is well placed to fend-off the potential competitive threat from western banks.

Throughout Central Europe, the move towards a market driven economy has gathered pace as state ownership and control over the banking sector has declined. In Poland, the traditional single tier banking sector of the National Bank has been replaced by the liberalisation of financial services within a new regulatory framework.

Climate of Change

At the heart of this has been the transformation of the National Bank of Poland into a western style Central Bank and a privatisation programme which has seen the creation of a host of new banks, including the initial formation of nine regional joint stock banks out of the old state bank's national network. Over the past five years, a fast rationalising banking sector has emerged which is acutely aware of the potential role and impact of western banks looking to enter Poland.

However, initial experience dampened enthusiasm for forming alliances with western companies. Today some of this has become cynicism for alliances with 'partners' from the west who have not met expectations.

There is also criticism of many computer companies and consultants who arrogantly push 'western' solutions without paying attention to the unique needs of Poland.

However, as the dust settles, some international computer companies and management consultants are gaining the respect of their local partners by acting as 'bridges' to the best of the west but then moulding them into relevant solutions which reflect the best of local practices. Such strategic partnerships are increasingly seen as offering the host financial institution a competitive advantage, enabling it to compete with foreign and other Polish banks. Bank Slaski is a case in point.

Based in the Slask region of Poland, Bank Slaski has bucked the trend of being overly cautious of western or foreign influences, instead seeing itself as part of the wider international community. It stands out as having embraced what can be learnt, before adapting and implementing a solution which reflects best practice for itself and for the Polish market.

Brunon Bartkiewicz, Vice President of Bank Slaski explains: "There are many aspects of the western retail banking industry that we seek to emulate here. We recognise that western-style business process re-engineering provides the opportunity to adopt new technology and work practices to reduce the size, as well as cost of the back office function, thereby optimising our investment in our people and their contact with customers.

"Our ambition is to make the focus on customer service key to everything that we do, thereby moving from a purely product focus to a market drive∗ sales and customer care culture. To do this we want to use the latest technology to provide multiple customer and account relationships which are easily accessible.

"A reflection of these aims is the objective to reduce back office costs and increase accounts-per-employee productivity. As we achieve this goal, we will jump at least two generations of technical development to make Bank Slaski one of the most advanced banks in Poland today."

(EUROPE) LTD.

Strategic Partnerships

To achieve its aims Bank Slaski realised that outside help would be of benefit if used in the right way. Brunon Bartkiewicz selected IDOM Consultants based in Geneva. After an extensive analysis of Bank Slaski's needs, IDOM produced a proposal for the way forward which was quickly followed by an invitation to tender. This was won by FIserv Europe, a key factor being FIserv's proven success in implementing its Comprehensive Banking System (CBS) worldwide in financial institutions of similar size and type to Bank Slaski.

FIserv was appointed to implement CBS across Bank Slaski's entire retail banking network and work commenced in May 1993. Eleven months later on April 1, 1994 and following rigorous pilot testing of CBS, (as translated and adapted for the Polish market), the first branch went live in Wadowice in the south of Poland. This early and rapid success has now been repeated in the important Bielsko Biala region as well as a number of key branches such as the main branch in Katowice, which is one of the largest of its kind in Poland. The 'roll out' continues and Bank Slaski intends to have 19 regions and over 60 branches fully operational by the end of 1995. This will firmly position the Bank at the forefront of Polish customer banking.

Service Benefits

FIserv's Comprehensive Banking Solution and the IBM AS/400 provide a powerful combination for modern high-volume processing which has brought Bank Slaski immediate benefits, including:

- Full support for Polish banking requirements

- Fast creation of new products

- High volume processing without lengthy end-of-days

- Automated National Bank reporting

- Accurate real time enquiries and reporting at branch level and/or head office

- Improved procedures enabling customers to be served from a single station without the need for going from one service point to another

- Automation of previously manual validation and approval procedures

- Comprehensive and fully automated support for Poland's complex lending administration requirements

- Sophisticated Cash Management support for corporate customers

- Membership of an international network of over 250 CBS users, spanning some 30 countries.

CBS DIVISION

> **❝ It is Bank Slaski's intention to provide a corporate service offering that major corporate customers, Polish or foreign, cannot afford to pass up ❞**
> Brunon Bartkiewicz

Bottom Line

As Brunon Bartkiewicz notes: "With many of our competitors still at the specification stage, we feel justifiably proud to be at the cutting edge of customer service and back office cost-efficiency. This would not have been possible without the support and commitment of FIserv".

Alex Groenendyk, President, CBS International, FIserv Inc notes: "Wary of over ambitious claims by western suppliers, Bank Slaski and IDOM sought a partnership with FIserv because of our proven, international track record. Wadowice showed how the system could work in Poland and ensured that the full scale installation would be able to handle all types of transactions, for all volumes. It has been one of the most rigorous on-site evaluations that FIserv has ever been asked to handle.

"CBS came through with flying colours at Bank Slaski and consequently we have learnt a great deal about providing solutions in Poland. We are now rolling the system out to the remainder of the Bank Slaski branch network. To ensure the smooth running of the project, a core team of FIserv personnel has been seconded to Bank Slaski. This ensures that our people and those of the bank work side by side, exploiting the system to its greatest potential. It also means that FIserv has created a strong team with considerable experience of implementing solutions in Poland."

Brunon Bartkiewicz concludes: "What did surprise us was how swiftly the users wanted to drop the former system which was running in parallel for an overlap period. This speaks volumes for how well the FIserv system has been received. At the same time the new system is already pointing to increased retail deposits from satisfied customers, whilst producing very real bottom-line savings from cost containment among back office staff.

Bank Slaski is looking closely at how best to use FIserv's specialist system for corporate cash management services. This is for large, often multi-national businesses operating in Poland which need and expect to get on line information about their accounts at their finger tips.

Just as Bank Slaski is now able to cross market multiple customer accounts, so it wishes to mirror this in the corporate market by giving business customers a comprehensive view of all their relationships with the Bank.

At the time of publication (January 1995), FIserv Europe's clients include four of central Europe's top 50 banks, plus a number of other major international financial organisations.

CBS Division, 5 Roundwood Avenue, Stockley Park, Uxbridge, Middlesex UB11 1AX
Tel: +44(01)81 899 2345 Fax: +44(01)81 899 2350 Telex: 290763 FIserv-G
Produced by Sector Public Relations, Cameo House, Bear Street, London WC2H 7AS on behalf of FIserv (Europe) Ltd.

KEY LEARNING POINTS

- The corporate brochure:
  - Find out as much as you can about the organisation first.
  - Must contain factual information about the organisation and what it offers to its customers.
  - Include short customer testimonials where possible.

- The newsletter:
  - Ensure style and tone are consistent throughout and appropriate to readership.
  - Customer (external) newsletters are more formal than staff (in-house) newsletters.
  - Stick to an editorial format.

- The case study:
  - Focus on the customer.
  - Use bullet points to emphasise the benefits the supplier has brought to the customer.
  - Include extensive and appropriate customer comment.

167

6
■ ■ ■

Writing sales letters

Purpose

The purpose of a sales letter (often called 'direct mail', but I prefer the non-jargonistic term) is to sell whatever you are offering in the letter.

The range of products and services sales letters offer is limitless; it would be no exaggeration to say there are probably no human needs, the satisfaction of which someone, somewhere, has not at some point tried to promote by means of the sales letter.

Today, there is a distinct tendency for sales letters to focus on selling *relationships* between the vendor and the customer, rather than selling a one-off product or service. This is not to say one-off selling no longer takes place, but the usual aim of the sales letter is nowadays to create a relationship between vendor and customer which will ideally lead to the customer being a customer for many years, and spending a considerable sum.

Examples of such 'relationship' products and services typically sold by means of sales letters are:

- Magazine subscriptions.
- Credit cards and charge cards.
- Investments, pensions and other financial services.
- Insurance.
- Subscriptions to 'limited editions' of objects of some (or at least some alleged) artistic merit.
- Correspondence courses.

The reason why sales letters tend to focus on these relationship products and services is primarily an economic one. Researching or buying in lists of potential customers, writing sales letters, stuffing them into envelopes, addressing the envelopes, taking them to the post office, franking or sticking stamps on them is expensive: **it is essential anyone contemplating doing this first works out exactly what the customer is worth, and does not proceed with the sales letter campaign unless the financial aspects make sense**.

Say, for example, you wanted to sell a product which costs the customer £19.99 and which gives you £10 profit per item (*after* paying for postage and packing). You may on the face of it decide that selling this product by means of sales letters (that is, by means of a direct mail campaign) makes sense.

You might work out that each mailing is going to cost you about 70 pence, including the cost of the envelope and the paper on which the letter is written, the stamp and with the cost of preparing, say, 2000 mailings, averaged out. Incidentally, this cost of 70 pence per mailing is just about the rock-bottom price for a mailing that only involves a one-page letter being placed into the envelope: if you want an enclosure such as a brochure to be included this would increase the cost considerably.

You might, in effect, say to yourself, 'yes, this makes sense. Two thousand people will hear about my product; each mailing costs me 70 pence, and every sale makes me £10. The quicker I get the mailing out, the better.'

Except that before you get going on your brilliant idea for a mailing you need to stop and face up to the practical realities. Extensive evidence from the marketing industry has shown that:

- About 40 percent of unsolicited mailings **do not even get opened**.
- Of those which do get opened, between 10 percent and 20 percent will be binned the moment the reader realises they are an unsolicited mailing.

In other words, **if 50 percent of the people to whom you sent the mailing even bother to read it, you will have done well**. The real cost of your mailing, per letter, is therefore not 70 pence at all, but £1.40, and this figure assumes the wildly improbable case that everyone who reads the mailing buys your product.

There is no accepted industry standard for the number of people who actually *respond* to a mailing by making a positive buying decision. The response rate will vary from 0 percent in the most unsuccessful cases to about 75 percent in the most successful cases.

One can say tentatively that a reasonably good response would be about five percent, which means that one in twenty of the people who bother to read your mailing buy what you are trying to sell them. If you got a five percent response to your mailing, each positive response would have cost you £28 (i.e. £1.40 x 20).

Result: financial disaster.

The truth is that unless you have a product to sell that is so remarkable the world will want to beat a path to your door – in which case you would be out of your mind only to charge £19.99 for it in the first place – it is simply not economically viable to use direct mail to sell a product which is only worth £10 to you per customer. This is the reason why most direct mail aims to set up a relationship between customer and vendor which will be worth many hundreds of pounds – or even quite possibly many thousands of pounds – to the vendor. The vendor can then handle a relatively low, or even extremely low, response rate.

So are there ways of improving the response rate?

Yes, there are. With 40 percent of your readers likely to bin the mailing without even opening it, there is obviously a strong case for you to take every step you can to prevent the reader realising it is an unsolicited mailing before actually opening the envelope.

With another 10 to 20 percent of readers likely to bin the envelope once they *do* realise it's an unsolicited mailing, it makes abundant sense for you to take every step to make them want to read it rather than bin it. And, once you've got them reading the mailing, **you must use every ounce of your ingenuity and persuasive power to make them want to read to the end of the letter, and to want to take up whatever you are offering them**.

In other words, you must write a stunning sales letter.

Typical readership

This chapter is about writing that stunning sales letter, rather than about doing all the accompanying marketing work. Still, it must be pointed out that you aren't going to have much success selling your range of extra-warm thermal underwear if your mailing list consists of the names and addresses of tribesmen in Equatorial Guinea.

The truth is that even if you write the best sales letter ever, your efforts will be wasted if your mailing list is not the best you can assemble.

By far the most successful mailing list, in terms of maximum likelihood of positive response, is a list of people who have bought from you already. They know you; they trust you; they are aware you can deliver what you promise and that your products will be good. You are, in effect, a brand, and people like to buy brands they have already found satisfactory.

My advice is that if possible you should always use a mailing list you have painstakingly built up yourself from giving customers satisfaction and – to use the phrase of the noted American business guru Paul Hawken – 'winning permission in the marketplace' by supplying what people want and to the quality they demand.

173

There is no doubt you will get a much better response from a few hundred customers who know and like you than from several thousand who don't know you and haven't yet had the opportunity to like you.

On the other hand, no business can grow unless it is able to win over complete strangers to what it has to sell. So there is no avoiding the need to use a 'cold' list at some point.

My advice is that you load your expenditure towards spending on research rather than quantity of names. Take the trouble to research the list thoroughly: even if this means making some telephone calls to potential names on the list. What you mustn't do is simply assume that just because you have a large number of names your mailing will be successful. In fact, it probably won't be if those names haven't been well-researched. In direct mail there is no safety in numbers, any more than there is for lemmings.

Imagine you are a photocopying lease bureau and are trying to sell new leases to customers. For a modest sum, you could buy a list of the names, addresses and telephone numbers of all the businesses in your region which are likely to need a photocopying machine. You might decide, for example, that this would be true of businesses with an annual turnover of more than £50,000. List-broking organisations will readily supply lists of businesses which qualify under criteria such as this and any other criteria you might specify.

So you have the list in your hands. Do you write off to them all at once? I suggest you don't.

The point is, the only businesses on that list who are *truly* potential customers for you are the ones who:

- Don't have a photocopier at all.
- Do have a photocopier on lease but whose leases are going to expire within (say) the next three months.

By telephoning the organisations you should be able to find out the ones to which the above two fundamental criteria apply. These are the organisations to which you should send your mailing.

I know: undertaking telephone research takes time and is expensive. If your initial list contains many thousands of names, it probably won't be realistic for you to ring them all up at once: you may need to focus on, say, one hundred at a time. Yet when you write to the ones you have selected, you know they will at least be in your market, and receptive to your sales message. And, as before, writing to thirty organisations who are receptive to your sales message is going to give you a much better response than writing to a hundred who aren't.

What you need to know about the product and/or organisation

The point that needs making here is that to write a good sales letter you need to know what makes the product and/or organisation *different from its competitors*. Of course, an in-depth knowledge of the product and the vendor won't do you any harm, either.

Blueprint

The fundamental problems of getting people to open your envelope in the first place, and getting them to read the enclosure even if they do open it, mean that before we look at how to write your stunning sales letter we need to see what we can do about those two problems.

The best way to make your recipient want to open your mailing is to prevent it looking like an unsolicited mailing at all. The way to achieve *that* effect is to personalise the letter by putting a person's name on the envelope (and in the salutation on the letter, of course) as well as the name and address of their organisation, **and to handwrite the envelope and put a stamp on it**.

By handwriting the envelope instead of typing it or using a label you immediately make the letter stand out from the crowd of what comes through the recipient's letterbox. The use of a stamp, rather than a franking-machine, complements this effect.

If you doubt these two techniques will work, consider whether *you* are more likely to open a handwritten, stamped envelope than one whose address or label has been typed, and one which is franked.

175

In fact, these two techniques are perfectly legitimate and fair. What is *neither* legitimate *nor* fair is to write 'personal' or 'private' on the letter. That's cheating, and will not in any way endear you to your recipient.

Even if your mailing is a large one, handwriting the envelope and sticking a stamp on it will be worthwhile. Many mailing agencies offer this service; true, at a higher price than standard mailings, but the exceptional always costs more money. And brings results.

There are other techniques for increasing the likelihood of the recipient actually opening your envelope. These techniques all depend on printing something on the outside of the envelope which is supposed to make the recipient want to look inside.

You will no doubt have seen this sort of thing in numerous unsolicited mailings you have received yourself: 'HAVE YOU WON ONE MILLION POUNDS? LOOK INSIDE TO FIND OUT', 'THIS WILL TRANSFORM YOUR LIFE', 'THE MOST EXCITING OFFER YOU WILL RECEIVE ALL YEAR'.

Inevitably, if you do look inside, you'll find you *haven't* won one million pounds, that the contents of the envelope *don't* transform your life, and that it *isn't* the most exciting offer you've received all year.

The point is that all these envelope-teasers have one fundamental drawback: they insult the recipient's intelligence. Most people are perfectly aware the mailing is a junk mailing, and no amount of teasers will convince them otherwise. Result: your letter is thrown unopened into the bin.

But your handwritten and stamped envelope has induced the recipient to open your envelope. How do you make him want to read your letter beyond giving it a cursory glance?

Answer: make the personalisation convincing, and make sure you put an incentive in the first sentence of your letter.

Most personalisations are not convincing. We have all seen those dreadful ones which start something like this:

Dear MR ESSINGER

This letter contains a very special offer, MR ESSINGER, for you and your family. MR ESSINGER, how would you like to spend two weeks of every year in your own French farmhouse, available during that period solely for the use of THE ESSINGER FAMILY?

Letters which start this way are so pitiful I sometimes wonder whether even the people who send them expect to get a reply. The personalisation device is ludicrously obvious, and there isn't an Essinger family in my house anyway, just me, two cats and two fishing-rods.

Probably the senders of this type of letter don't expect to get many replies. They do, however, know there are enough people out there who *will* respond to this kind of mailing, and that the cost of two weeks, in perpetuity, in a French farmhouse will justify the mailing even if only one in two hundred recipients respond.

You have to do better. There's no point personalising the letter if the personalisation looks insincere and absurd; nor is there – as we have seen – much point sending the letter out at all if you haven't done your research.

I suggest you restrict the personalisation of the letter to putting the name and address of the recipient at the top and to using the name of the recipient in the salutation. With any luck the recipient will then read at least the first paragraph of your letter.

Of course, you shouldn't hesitate to use more sophisticated personalisation techniques as and when they become available: just make sure that the technique keeps the personalisation subtle rather than glaringly obvious.

So, now you have to win the reader's attention and hold it throughout the entire letter.

Despite the mystique (and enormous incomes) which some expert writers of direct mail letters manage to acquire for themselves, there is not in fact any mystery to the secret of writing a successful sales letter. Instead, there are six fundamental rules which you must follow. These rules are:

1. Write your letter from the point of view of the reader's needs rather than your own wishes and hopes.

2. Write to the reader as though you're talking to a friend.

3. Keep the letter no more than one side of paper in length.

4. Put an incentive in the first paragraph. The incentive will sometimes be an offer of a specific gift or financial reward, but it can simply be a *benefit*, if the benefit is good enough.

5. Make the letter as concise and to the point as you possibly can.

6. Don't use jargon: that is, words and phrases which mean something to you but which your reader may not immediately understand. If you need to mention technical points in your letter, do this briefly and make sure the points are readily comprehensible. Of course, the need to avoid jargon does *not* mean you should talk down to your reader.

Obeying these six rules will ensure the letter is written for the reader, not for you. Which is, after all, what writing for a stranger is all about.

✍ **EXAMPLE 32**

T I M E T O U R S PLC
Chronos House
Reading
Berkshire
Eurocode UK/RD/1A

A. Prospect Esq.
'Dunroamin'
Suburbia Drive
Surbiton
Surrey

May 1 2025

Dear Mr Prospect

Would you like to hunt a Tyrannosaurus Rex? Wander through the Hanging Gardens of Babylon? Discuss religion with Jesus Christ? Stop Alfred the Great burning the cakes? Act in William Shakespeare's *Hamlet* – with William Shakespeare? Drink bourbon with Humphrey Bogart and Ingrid Bergman?

Now, for literally the first time in history, you can.

You'll have read about the remarkable discovery United States researchers have made: that equipment developed to create artificial gravity also enables effective and totally safe time dilation. As a result, travel to the past is now – amazingly – possible.

Timetours plc is the only company in the UK to have been granted a licence to use time dilation equipment for recreational purposes.

What does this mean to you? It means that you, Sally, Rebecca and Peter can enjoy the holiday of a lifetime. For Rebecca and Peter it'll be even more than a holiday: it'll be the most tremendous educational experience they can imagine.

The time dilation equipment we use has been tested to full European Federation standards and is perfectly safe. Your inclusive holiday price includes the cost of all clothing and equipment, and a training seminar in avoiding time paradoxes. The only extra charge is made for currency that is geographically and chronologically appropriate.

All this for as little as one million Euro-yen per person.

Use the coupon below to send off for our illustrated brochure, *Time and Time Again*, and see for yourself how you could be off on a time adventure in no time at all.

Best wishes

N. Bonaparte (Managing Director)

179

KEY LEARNING POINTS

- ■ Do your sums first and make sure they make sense.

- ■ Research your mailing list carefully.

- ■ Handwrite your envelopes and use stamps.

- ■ Use personalisation subtly.

- ■ Write with the reader's interests in mind.

7

...

Writing speeches and presentations

Purpose

The purpose of a speech or presentation is to convey information to an audience in such a way that they want to absorb it. A speech will usually be presented to a fairly large audience at a conference, seminar or similar event; a presentation will usually be made to a strictly limited audience – such as to the people at an organisation who are responsible for choosing a new marketing or advertising agency.

Should a speech or presentation be written down at all?

Some experienced speakers would say no, and would argue that speeches and presentations should be prepared purely in note form, thereby giving the speaker the chance to make the speech come alive during the event itself.

Certainly nothing is duller than a speaker reading out a speech in a monotonic voice which makes no concession to one simple, brutal fact: **you can't convey information to people in a speech or presentation unless you first entertain them**.

Let me elaborate on this point before returning to the question of whether or not a speech or presentation should be scripted.

The delivery of a speech or presentation is inseparable, *absolutely inseparable*, from its content. You can no more effect a separation between the delivery and content of a speech than you can expect a cinema audience, if the projector breaks down, to be satisfied by each being lent a copy of the screenplay of the film they were planning to see.

This is why the names of the stars get far more emphasis in a cinema poster than the name of the screenwriter: the audience attaches more importance to the actor's performance of the dialogue than to the dialogue itself (although good dialogue helps, too).

Most commercial organisations have little or no understanding of this fundamental point. They continue to allow senior managers to deliver speeches at conferences and seminars, even though the managers in question – for all their commercial ability – have no talent for public speaking and will bore their audience rigid. They continue to allow a presentation team to consist of people who may be great at getting on with the work they will win if the presentation succeeds, but who have no real idea how to deliver the presentation so that the likelihood of winning the business is maximised.

Think of the conferences and seminars you have attended as a delegate. What percentage of the speeches interested you beyond the first ten minutes? During what percentage of the speeches did your mind *not* wander to thinking of that video you saw last night, your lover, what's for lunch, your financial position?

Zero percent? Five percent? Any more than five percent and you'll deserve an entry in the *Guinness Book of Records* under the category of Least Distracted Conference Delegate.

I suggest you should *only* speak at conferences and seminars if you believe (and have evidence for the belief) you have a talent for public speaking. If not, find someone else at your organisation to deliver your speech. If you can't, give serious consideration to the possibility of hiring an actor to give your speech. The vast majority of actors are out of work; finding a really able actor to present your speech is easy. You will, however, have to convince the theatrical agency you contact that you are bona fide and creditworthy.

183

Using an actor to present a speech at a conference or seminar may seem unrealistic to you; it isn't. An increasing number of organisations are seeing the sense in doing it. For example, Reuters – the world's largest vendor of financial information and computer-based financial trading systems – regularly uses actors to present its annual results.

You can't use actors in presentations: the audience will, reasonably enough, want to meet at the presentation the people who would handle their business, or at least the bosses of the people who would handle their business.

However, you *can* do your utmost to ensure that the members of the presentation team know how to present or will receive training in this if they don't, and that they have thoroughly *rehearsed* their presentation before they deliver it.

Incidentally, if you are using visual aids in a speech or presentation, keep them straightforward and to the point. Avoid overcomplex visual aids; it's too easy for your audience to be put off by them and wind up focusing more on the visual aids than on the content of the speech or presentation.

As for whether or not the speech or presentation should be scripted, my advice is that you should **script a speech but avoid scripting a presentation**.

If you don't script a speech there is a serious danger the speaker will dry up, which is about the worst thing a speaker can do short of passing out or breaking wind. I once attended a major international conference where a delegate from a leading global management consultancy dried up for about one minute in the middle of a speech: that minute seemed to last several centuries.

Almost as bad as drying up is waffling or wandering off the point. Your audience will not be tolerant of either. Make no mistake: if you don't hold their interest they'll stop listening to you, and some may even walk out. After all, they're paying good money to hear you: they want (and are entitled to get) value for money.

You could write down your speech in note form. This can be a good solution if you're an experienced speaker and you know what you are doing. Be warned, though, that notes which seemed so full and detailed when your wrote them can seem horribly sparse and unhelpful when you're staring at them in front of an audience of two hundred people and desperately trying to think what on earth to say next.

My solution is to write out the script of the speech in full, **but not to be afraid of enlarging on the script as you present it**, as long as the extra material is strictly relevant.

As for a presentation, if it is a shortish one and you are spreading the burden of the presentation among several people, there's no reason why everybody shouldn't learn what they have to say by heart, perhaps cueing themselves with a visual aid. Otherwise, use notes, but make sure you know exactly what you mean by a particular note. Don't script the whole thing: it'll be far too unspontaneous and forced. The only possible exception is where you are all so polished that – like the presenters of *Blue Peter* – you can deliver a script in a completely natural way. Even so, I still tend to think you should avoid scripting the entire presentation. After all, your audience – unlike the audience of *Blue Peter* – will want to ask questions.

By the way, in a presentation **every member of the team presenting must take part**. If they're not part of the presenting team, don't take them along. If you do, they'll feel (and, more important, look) like gate-crashers.

Typical audience

This will depend entirely on the nature of the speech or presentation and the circumstances under which it is presented. Above all, remember that your audience – like the hypothetical readers we have been imagining throughout this book – will be high-calibre people with a low boredom threshold.

What you need to know about the product and/or organisation

You need to know as much about both of these as you can reasonably find out. When you present a speech or presentation you are in effect an ambassador for your organisation or client, and ambassadors have to know what they are talking about.

Blueprint

When you write a speech you are writing a *script*: that is, words to be spoken aloud. Your speech should read exactly as it will be spoken: with the same idiomatic style and 'audience-friendly' tone the spoken word ought to embody.

A principal consequence of this is that while the same requirements for conciseness, precision, and energy and drama of expression apply as when you are writing material to be read, there are some important additional rules you need to follow. These rules are:

1. You should pay even more attention to using familiar words than you do when writing copy that is not deliberately designed to be read aloud.

2. You should feel free to use idiomatic expressions: which should not, however, deteriorate into slang.

3. You should generally avoid long sentences. For the purposes of a speech a long sentence can be taken to mean one with more than three dependent clauses. This doesn't mean you should avoid long sentences completely, but that you should only use one where the sense of what you are trying to say makes it unavoidable.

4. You should make your paragraphs shorter than you would make them if you were writing copy not designed to be read aloud. Paragraphs in a script for a speech should never be more than two sentences long, and the general rule is to use one paragraph for each sentence.

The reason for making paragraphs short in a script for a speech is that this makes the speech sound more natural when it is read aloud.

5. Use the same contractions of words in the script you use in everyday speech. Say 'don't' rather than 'does not', 'isn't' rather than 'is not', 'hasn't' rather than 'has not' and so on.

6. Make liberal use of bullet-points to deal with lists of any kind, whether these are lists of features, of points or of anything else. Using bullet-points helps the audience to focus on the items in the list, and also gives the audience useful pauses in the flow of the main speech, thereby helping to keep their attention.

Finally, two tactical points about speeches.

1. Don't automatically assume you need to use slides. A good speaker can employ gesture, voice inflection, changes in expressiveness and pace, and (of course) sheer quality of the speech to dramatise what he is saying; slides are a poor substitute for this. They are less interesting than many speakers imagine, and usually slow the pace of a speech to a serious extent.

If you must use slides, don't use too many. One slide for every three minutes of speech is enough. Don't put too many words on the slides, either: just the main points you want to discuss. I don't recommend you put more than 100 words on any one slide. If you do, there's a severe danger your audience will read the slide instead of listening to you.

2. Start the presentation by telling your audience you will be handing out or making available copies of the full script of your speech once you have delivered it. If members of an audience know that this will be available at the end, they won't spend time trying to write notes when they should be listening to what you are saying next.

Many conference and seminar organisers ask for copies of the speech (or notes) before the event starts. If you are asked for this, supply it but *don't* let the event organiser make the copy available to delegates until *after* you have delivered your speech. If delegates have your speech on their laps while you are delivering it they will often concentrate on the speech in front of them rather than you. Even worse, they may not come to listen to you at all.

✍ EXAMPLE 33

This is the start of a speech I wrote for one of my clients, which supplies banking software. I have made certain small deletions from the speech to avoid identifying the client.

Good morning.

In the next 45 minutes I'd like to take a look at the strategic issues surrounding plastic bank cards, the cards themselves, and the general nature of the plastic card market. By the way, a full copy of this speech will be available after I've spoken.

As most of you will know, we are in the process of launching a major new card management product. I'd like to say, right at the outset, that those of you who fear that this presentation will merely be a 45-minute sales pitch for our new product can relax.

Although I'll be summarising the major features of the product later in the speech, my overriding aim is to look at the kind of conceptual issues that have made us so keen to launch our card management product in the first place.

You see, I think it's a mistake to do what many commentators do, and regard plastic cards in isolation, as though they were something self-contained that somehow existed independently of the banks which issue them and the public who use them. We need to regard them in a more holistic way: as an integral part of what might be termed the retail banking proposition.

What do I mean by this, exactly?

Well, what I'd say is that plastic cards should be seen as the meeting-point of two needs.

These needs are:

- The customer's need to obtain banking services.

- The institution's need to deliver banking services to the largest number of customers and with maximum profitability.

Let's look at these needs in a little more detail.

In the highly automated, dynamic, exciting and really quite colourful retail banking world of today, it's all to easy to forget that it wasn't so long ago when a financial institution was about as dynamic, exciting and colourful an entity as a lump of stone.

Many of them, indeed, were housed in headquarters built out of stone, and although these institutions were of course commercial businesses, they very much had the look of government departments.

They behaved rather like government departments, too; treating customers with cold respect rather than warmth; seeing customers as people who were privileged to do business with the bank; offering loans and deposit facilities to certain customers as though the bank were doing these people a big favour.

Not surprisingly, once people were accepted by a bank and had begun a relationship with it – no matter how cold and distant that relationship might be – they weren't likely to want to change to another bank, and experience the problems of getting accepted by the bank all over again.

Enormous changes in the public perception of financial institutions have altered the face of banking over the past twenty years or so.

The days when banks were able to regard their customers as privileged to do business with the bank are gone forever – at least in those countries with developed banking infrastructures.

Basically, what we have seen in these countries have been sweeping social changes which have resulted in people becoming aware of the dynamics of consumer choice, and the overall power of the consumer, in a way that was never previously the case.

Initially these changes applied mainly to the purchase of consumer goods. However, it was inevitable that changing attitudes towards the purchase of consumer goods would before long also affect the purchase of banking services, and this is precisely what has happened.

For example, here in the United Kingdom, many people now hold accounts with more than one financial institution, or more than one account at the same institution. A typical scenario would be for a person to have a bank account for writing cheques and for paying in his or her salary, and a building society account for holding savings on deposit.

However, this is only one type of scenario; many people prefer to use a current account operated by a building society, and keep their savings in one of the society's other accounts: typically one that pays higher interest.

Furthermore, we in the UK, as with people in all Western European countries, tend to be financially pretty knowledgeable – certainly far more financially knowledgeable than was the case twenty years ago – and extremely demanding of our financial institutions. Most of us are perfectly prepared to change from one financial institution to another if we believe it will give us better service.

189

In this scenario, where customers often have more than one account, and are financially knowledgeable and aware that financial institutions are competing for their business, any retail financial institution which wishes to compete successfully in the marketplace has got to be as competitive and customer-conscious as a market-stall owner who sells umbrellas when it rains and sunglasses when it's sunny.

But not only have customer expectations of their financial institutions changed, the nature of the customers themselves has also changed.

The major changes I'm talking about here are:

- People travel in their own countries on leisure and business much more than they ever have before.

- People travel internationally on leisure and business much more than they ever have before.

- People tend to move jobs and move house more than they did before.

- People expect their financial institution to seem eager for their business.

- People expect the process of handling their personal finances and paying for things to have some excitement attached to it.

- Young people – say, up to the age of 24 – have far more

spending power than they have ever had before, and expect institutions to offer services and facilities which will appeal directly to them.

■ Most people are familiar with electronic banking and like using electronic banking facilities. For an ever-increasing proportion of people, the electronic banking facilities *are* the bank.

I could talk about these changes in the nature of the customer for all the 45 minutes I've had allotted to me, but there isn't time.

Suffice it to say that customers' needs from financial institutions have become extremely complex, and immensely difficult to meet.

190

Using gimmicks

Once you gain experience in writing speeches, you can some-times use certain gimmicks to increase the dramatic impact of a particular speaker.

For example, a couple of years ago a bank approached me to write a speech for one of their senior managers. I met him, and found him to be a dynamic character who looked as though he easily had the strength of character to hold an audience. How-ever, the speech would be arguing a particularly abstruse, tech-nical case; I felt that anything which could increase its dramatic appeal would be most helpful.

I therefore wrote a speech in the form of a barrister's argument, with all the pompous – but nonetheless dramatically effective – 'barrister-speak' such as 'I maintain', 'with respect', 'if I may say,' and, finally, 'I rest my case', included. I also suggested the organ-isation borrow a barrister's wig, and that the senior manager deliver the speech in the wig.

He did. It worked.

KEY LEARNING POINTS

- **Entertain your audience.**
- **Script speeches, don't script presentations.**
- **Scripts must sound authentically like the spoken word.**
- **Slides are not always necessary.**

8
■ ■ ■

Writing advertising copy

Purpose

The purpose of advertising copy is to make your target audience – which can mean readers, viewers or listeners – want to become involved with the advertiser in some way, whether by purchasing products on offer, or by being more inclined towards the organisation.

Three distinct types of advertising are usually recognised. These are:

■ **Consumer advertising:** this is directed at consumers of products and services purchased by people for consumption in their personal lives. An important sub-section of consumer advertising concerns that for products known in the marketing business as fast-moving consumer goods (commonly abbreviated to fmcg). These are typically food, healthcare, cleaning, petfood and general domestic products – usually organised into brands – which have a high turnover and which occupy most of the floorspace in a supermarket.

■ **Business-to-business advertising:** as the name implies, this advertises products and services used by businesses. Products advertised range across a vast range of industrial and commercial sectors.

■ **Corporate advertising:** this is directed at increasing the general awareness of an organisation among the general public and/or among other, specific publics which the organisation wishes to target.

Advertising is a global industry worth many billions of dollars annually. A vast amount of effort and expenditure is devoted by organisations and their advertising agencies to maximise the effectiveness of advertising. The power of advertising – particular fmcg advertising – to influence spending habits is widely recognised, and there is no doubt that a good advertising campaign can dramatically increase the success of a product. Many brands have been charged through their advertising with a glamour and mystique which is often almost ludicrously at odds with the actual nature of the product.

Typical audience

All advertising activity requires careful planning. The most brilliant advertisement in the world will not boost sales of a product or service if it does not reach the right audience. For an advertising campaign to achieve maximum success, every element of it – from identification of target audience, choice of the medium or media used to reach that audience, and quality and power of the advertisement itself – must be right.

Ultimately, selecting the most appropriate medium or media is a numbers game, with organisations, or their advertising agencies, analysing the total readership, number of listeners or number of viewers which an advertisement will reach, and dividing this by the total cost of preparing and publicising the advertisement.

For example, the most expensive advertising slot in British television is the commercial break during *News at Ten*. The total cost of making a 20-second advertisement, and paying for the TV time to broadcast it, is unlikely to be less than £30,000 and may be much more for the most ambitious type of corporate advertisement (of course, this cost can be regarded in terms of being spread over all the slots where the advertisement is broadcast).

However, *News at Ten* has an average nightly audience of about 10 million, and while these will not all watch the commercial break (some will switch channels, leave the room, or take their eyes off the screen for one reason or another), the number of viewers reached will still be regarded by many organisations as amply justifying the expenditure.

If your organisation is planning a major advertising campaign you need in-depth professional advice, whether from a large agency or from one of the many hundreds of highly skilled freelance advertising agents/consultants who are available in most areas of the country. I mention freelancers because:

- Many of them are extremely talented and will give you excellent value for money.
- A large agency (by which I mean the better-known ones which feature regularly on the pages of the advertising industry journal *Campaign*) will probably only be interested in you if your annual media expenditure is likely to be in the region of at least £250,000. Most advertising agencies nowadays tend to work on a fee rather than a

195

commission basis. However, unless you are a serious player, the agency will not be able to charge fees that will give it a healthy profit on the time its staff devote to your account.

What you need to know about the product and/or organisation

This is where things become difficult. The point is that what you need to know about the product and/or organisation to write a successful advertisement about it is *not* the same at all as the detailed commercial information relating to such matters as production, raw material supply, inventory control, accounting, management decision-making, and all the other areas which you need to get the product produced in the first place, or to make the organisation run successfully.

Advertising is something else. Advertising is about presenting your product and/or organisation to customers in the most imaginative and energetic way you can.

Frankly, it is difficult – and often impossible – for someone on the inside of an organisation to do this. Such a person will usually be too close to the product and/or organisation to generate the necessary level of objectivity about what the product and/or organisation *really* has to offer.

Blueprint

It is for this reason that when it comes to writing advertising copy, my general advice is *not* to try to write your own copy, but to obtain the assistance of a skilled freelance copywriter, and give him or her a detailed briefing about the product and organisation.

You really need to help the copywriter know about your product and organisation if you want him to produce some great advertisements for you. But isn't this a contradiction of my belief that if someone is too close to the organisation they can't produce advertising for it?

No, because even though the copywriter will want to know as much as possible about what you are offering to your customers, *he will remain an outsider*, and therefore able to retain the kind of distance necessary to write advertisements that work.

Many freelance advertising agents/consultants offer a copywriting service themselves; all will know of someone who offers this service: many will work with the writer on a sub-contractor basis. You can find listings of regional advertising agencies and freelance agents in your local *Yellow Pages*, but if you are above all looking for a copywriter, you should consult *Campaign*, which has listings of these people.

Do not immediately hire the first copywriter with whom you make contact. Instead, talk to three or four and ask them to send you references, examples of work already completed and details of their fees. Take up references (regrettably, some freelancers in all fields claim to have done work they didn't actually do) and select the person who seems to provide the best mix of talent and cost.

If, despite the above, you are adamant about writing your own advertising copy – or if you are a marketing consultant eager to add the skill of advertising copyewriting to your repertoire – you should spend as much time as you can afford studying advertisements in print, on radio and on television. What does the advertisement set out to achieve? Do you think it achieves it? If not, how could it have been written so as to achieve its objectives more fully?

197

When you finally start writing your own advertisements, keep the following rules firmly in mind:

1. Identify the target audience's problems or needs and make these the focus of the entire advertisement.

People buy things because they want to solve a problem. This problem can take numerous forms, but generally it stems from the following motivations:

- To satisfy hunger.
- To satisfy thirst.
- To keep warm and comfortable.
- To feel better if they are feeling ill.
- To be more sexually attractive.
- To have somewhere pleasant to live.
- To obtain more money.

- To make more of their leisure time.

- To feel more important.

- (At work) to carry out their job more easily and effectively.

This is not a complete list of human motivation; I have left out some motivations, such as the desire to feel closer to God, which do not have obvious implications for advertising; but it is pretty comprehensive. By definition, whatever you are offering your customers will meet a need, and it's a fair chance this need will be somewhere on that list.

The entire logic and thrust of your advertisement should be geared around meeting the customer need you have identified.

2. Immediately promise the customer something helpful to meet their need.

You must get down to business right away, and establish the fundamental proposition of your advertisement – what you are offering the customer to meet their need – right upfront.

Ideally what you have to offer should be *new*. As poor, deluded human beings, hope does indeed spring eternally in our breasts, and we never cease to believe that something new will be better than what we've had before. Never mind that in many cases something new is actually worse than what we had before; we still go on believing that what is new will be better.

So offer your customers something new, even if it means revamping the product or making cosmetic changes to it. New is still beautiful, at least in the customer's eyes.

By the way, if you can combine the basic proposition of the advertisement with some sort of *incentive*, so much the better.

3. Sell as hard as possible.

This is an advertisement, not a subtle thoughtpiece article. It's the hard sell that is required here, so give your readers what they expect to find.

True: high-profile corporate advertisements do not attempt an overt hard sell, but often appear to strive more to get the customer in a particular mood. Yet if you look closely, through the beautiful cinematography and underneath the tones of the popular classical music the agency has borrowed from some composer who has been dead so long not even his descendants will receive a fee, the hard sell won't be far away. All advertising is about selling, so enjoy it.

4. Make sure the audience is given a means of responding.
For an fmcg product this will be easy enough; they'll be aware they just need to go into their supermarkets. The right way to respond to advertisements for other products and services will be almost equally obvious; but if the response method isn't obvious, make it so, by including a telephone number and/or address. If it's a print advertisement you can of course incorporate a coupon into the advertisement.

5. Write in as focused, concise and energetic a method as you possibly can.
There is simply no room for even a word of waffle. Your audience isn't interested in any pompous corporate statement, either; all they're interested in is how you can meet their needs.

6. Do your best to think of a good slogan, but don't panic if you can't.
Great slogans like 'Players please' and 'Diamonds are forever' are minor works of genius; you can't expect that level of inspiration to hit you every day. Remember, in any case, that the essence of a great slogan isn't its clever play on words or its simplicity, but that with wit and brevity, it summarises all the benefits of what you have to offer.

7. Start your advertisement with some eye-catching statement which, even if isn't a great slogan, does achieve this effect of summarising your entire proposition. I mention how to start the advertisement last of all because until you've absorbed the other six rules you've no business writing your advertisement in the first place.

I'm not supplying an example of a piece of advertising copy. There are so many ways in which a good advertisement can be written that I don't see any instructional benefit in singling out one particular example. Besides, all you have to do to see some examples is to switch on your television or buy a newspaper. Instead of supplying you with an example, I urge you again to get into the habit of looking critically at advertisements and doing your utmost to work out how you would have done better.

I hope you will.

KEY LEARNING POINTS

■ **Plan the advertising process carefully.**

■ **Get professional advice.**

■ **Don't try to write your own copy – use a copywriter.**

■ **Focus advertisements entirely on the target audience's needs.**

■ **Advertising is about selling.**

■ **Ensure audience knows how to respond.**

■ **Start with an eye-catching summary statement.**

9
■ ■ ■

Revision

Differences between amateur and professional writers

Revising your work effectively

Good marketing copy is not written, it is rewritten.

The only way – absolutely the *only* way – to become an expert at writing marketing copy is to develop a vicious, merciless, incorruptible ability to criticise your work. You must improve your work until it is as good as you can possibly make it.

In writing, as in many other areas of human expertise, the difference between the professional and the amateur lies partly in the degree of commitment, dedication and self-criticism they bring to the task.

The surest sign of amateurs is that they are unable to deal with criticism of their work. Criticism either devastates them or angers them. Oh, they may hand you their work with the instruction to *be as critical as you like*, but they're not looking for criticism, they're looking for praise.

This is why going to an amateur writing circle is such a dismal experience: the members' agenda isn't directed at doing everything they can to improve their work, including sweating over it all night if need be. No, what they want is praise.

Never mind that praise for work which is incompetent and dull is about as valuable as an acceptance letter from a vanity publisher: the praise is what they want. Incidentally, hundreds of amateur writers combine the vice of having a desperate yearning for praise with that of having more money than sense. Vanity publishers make an extremely good living.

Some years ago I went to hear a lecture given by the playwright, actor and director Steve Berkoff. Berkoff is a man of great talents; plays of his such as *East* and *Decadence* are fiestas of energy and contain language so dramatic and powerful it shoots you up into the stratosphere, like a rocket. He's a brilliant actor, too, starring in most of his plays, and he tends to steal the show in the popular films in which he appears: most notably *Beverly Hills Cop*, where he turned in a scintillating portrait of villainy.

During the lecture, which was about the art of theatre, Berkoff defined the difference between professional actors and amateur actors.

He characterised the difference as being that after a show, the professional actors are weary with exhaustion and the audience is cheering; whereas after an amateur show, the actors are cheering and the audience is weary with exhaustion.

All right: it's an exaggeration. I've seen amateur plays which leave you cheering, but in broad terms Berkoff's point is valid.

And what is in a large degree true of theatre is even more true of writing. Amateur writing leaves you weary; even assuming you're able to finish reading it: professional writing leaves you cheering. Amateur writers write to please themselves, professional writers write to please strangers.

The fundamental proposition of this book has been that the ability to write to a professional standard stems less from inherent talent – which you don't know whether you possess until you've learnt to write professionally, anyway – than from a determination to take writing seriously and a real willingness to learn how to do it more effectively.

Here, I add three final elements to the mix of what constitutes a professional writer:

■ you must be **determined to take your writing seriously**,

■ you must have a real **willingness to learn**,

■ you must **revise your work until it shines**.

Revision does not mean idly replacing the odd word with a synonym, it doesn't mean cutting the occasional sentence or fiddling around with your work in an indecisive way. It means treating a draft of your writing with aggressive, vicious critical energy that is as sharp as a kitchen knife and deadly as a tiger. You must have the guts – and believe me, it *does* take guts – to look at the work in front of you as if it were something written by someone else: someone you don't care about in the least, indeed, someone you positively dislike. Then, when you're in that frame of mind, attack that work from every side and make it better.

In Example 3 in Chapter One I deliberately composed a bad piece of writing to show how careful attention to detail can dramatically improve bad writing: can, in fact, convert a piece of amateurish writing into something professional. I don't intend to do that again in this chapter; by this stage in our journey together it would be an insult to your intelligence. Besides,

203

there's something profoundly silly about writing in a deliberately bad fashion: a bit like arriving at a Buckingham Palace garden party wearing only your underpants.

Instead, here are my rules for revising your work effectively.

1. If you've handwritten your first draft, get it word-processed. Ideally do this yourself to have another stab at your work right away.

2. Once it's on the screen (if you wrote it onto the word processor this will be the first stage of your revision process), read through it quickly, correcting it where you can for typos, spelling mistakes and obvious clumsiness of expression. Don't spend too long on this stage, however.

3. Print out the draft onto paper.

4. **Make sure at least one night elapses between writing your first draft and revising your work. The night will give you distance from your work.** A longer period of time between writing the first draft and revising your work will be even better, but you may not have this.

5. Revise your work with all the self-critical power you can muster. Write your corrections in hand on the hard copy.

6. When you've done that, call the work up on the screen, put all the revisions in, print out another hard copy and revise *that* with the same aggression before even thinking of showing it to anyone else.

As for the revision process itself, your fundamental task is to make your writing more interesting, more concise and more alive. I can't tell you exactly how to do that; it's a skill only practice and experience can help you improve.

I can, however, guide you on certain aspects of your writing to which you ought to pay particular attention when you revise your work. I have already covered many of these points earlier in the book.

When you revise your work, take care to:

- Cut any words, phrases or sentences not essential to your meaning.

- Replace abstract words with words that summon up concrete images.

- Rewrite expressions that *tell* the reader something into dramatic expressions which give the reader interesting sensory information about a specific example of what you are discussing.

- Delete all adverbs. If this leaves a conceptual gap in the copy, rewrite to replace the adverb with a dramatic image.

- Delete all adjectives not essential to your meaning.

- Replace a long word with a shorter word wherever this is possible.

- Rewrite any passive construction into an active construction wherever possible.

- Chop a lengthy sentence into a succession of shorter sentences wherever you can do this without compromising the meaning.

- Make sure you are using the colon or semi-colon to the fullest extent to create a dramatic tension in your sentences.

- Where a sentence consists of two clauses joined by 'and', see if rewriting the two clauses as two sentences without the 'and' improves the expression. If it does, rewrite in this way.

- Delete the word 'that' wherever it is not essential.

- Delete the word 'which' wherever it is not essential.

- Delete 'which is/which are' and 'who is/who are' wherever they are not essential.

- Use contractions (e.g. 'isn't' for 'is not', 'doesn't' for 'does not') wherever this makes the writing read better.

- Make sure all your similes and metaphors are completely original. Don't use *any* you have read in someone else's writing.

- Replace all foreign words and Latin/Greek phrases with their English equivalents.

- Only write 'he or she' once; thereafter use 'he'. Whatever fans of the politically correct say, 'he or she' looks awful. If you wish, briefly explain that 'he' implies 'he or she'. Alter-

205

natively, you can sometimes avoid the problem by making your hypothetical person plural and using the non sexually discriminatory pronoun 'they'.

■ Break any of the rules I have suggested in this book rather than write something hideous.

KEY LEARNING POINTS

■ Be your own harshest critic.

■ Revise your copy at least twice before showing it to anyone else.

■ Put your work away overnight before correcting it.

Beyond the blueprints

■ ■ ■

L earning to write is a never-ending story. It is a voyage without a final destination, for you can never completely master the art and science of writing; all you can do is work hard at it and get better. If that happens, you will find you are welcomed at your ports of call, and that at those ports you leave work behind which people will remember; work which will warm the cockles of your heart as you sail, alone, to the next port that lies on the other side of the horizon.

Beyond the blueprints you *are* alone, for ultimately there are no rules about writing, only skills and tips you learn as you work at it. You must commit yourself, with all your energy and courage, to ransacking the recesses of your mind in order to put words down that thrill your reader or audience. Learning that commitment is, in the end, the only rule that matters.

I started this book during the great heatwave of the summer of 1995, during which Britain was blessed – or, if you were a water company executive, cursed – with days hotter than anything recorded since the seventeenth century. I finish this book today on a bright, warm day in autumn, when the lakeside beckons me to one last try for a tench or a carp before the lake grows cold and the pike season begins.

I started this book with a fierce determination to give you everything I have learnt about writing since I first haltingly wrote my name with a pencil; I finish it feeling there is nothing I have kept secret from you, and that now the time has come for me to write something which is in no way instructional. For there is a time for giving advice, and a time for practising one's profession.

Appendix:
List of numbered examples

■ ■ ■

Number	Topic Illustrated
1	the need for a forceful message
2	brevity of expression
3	conciseness of expression
4	Anglo-Saxon/French words
5	informal/formal language
6	the need to be specific
7	actual spoken language
8	over-long sentences
9/10	well-formed long sentences
11	clumsy writing
12	bullet-points
13	poor capitalisation
14	proper use of the comma
15	dynamic use of the semi-colon
16	dynamic use of the dash
17	showing rather than telling
18	use of the dramatic image
19	starting a technical article
20/21	use of dynamic detail

Index

■ ■ ■

213